Sustainable and affordable housing

RE-INVENT
REUSE AND TRANSFORMATION IN LACATON & VASSAL'S ARCHITECTURE

Massimo Faiferri

CONTENTS

Reinventing the world   **6**

- House, Cap Ferret   **28**
- Latapie House, Floirac   **34**
- Tour Bois le Prêtre, Paris   **40**
- Transformation of 530 dwellings, Bordeaux   **46**
- Housing transformation, Saint-Nazaire   **52**
- Social housing, Mulhouse   **58**
- 96 dwellings, Chalon-sur-Saône   **64**
- 59 dwellings, Neppert gardens, Mulhouse   **70**
- Student and social housing, Ourcq-Jaurès, Paris   **76**
- Management Sciences University, Bordeaux   **82**
- School of architecture, Nantes   **88**
- Polyvalent Theater, Lille   **94**
- FRAC Nord-Pas de Calais, Dunkerque   **100**
- Palais de Tokyo, Paris   **108**

Seeking reality; *interview with Lacaton & Vassal*   **114**

Anne Lacaton
born in France in 1955. Graduated from the School of architecture of Bordeaux in 1980.
Diploma in Urban Planning at the university of Bordeaux in 1984.
Professor at ETH in Zurich since 2017.
Visiting professor at the University of Madrid, Master Housing 2007-2013, at the EPFL Lausanne, 2004, 2006, 2010-11 and 2017, University of Florida, Ivan Smith Studio in 2012, University of NY-Buffalo, Clarkson Chair in 2013, at the Pavillon Neuflize OBC-Palais de Tokyo, Paris, in 2013-2014, at Harvard GSD : Kenzo Tange 2011 & Design critic 2015, at TU Delft, sem 2016-17.

Jean Philippe Vassal
born in Casablanca, Morocco in 1954. Graduated from the school of architecture of Bordeaux in 1980.
Worked as urban planner in Niger (West Africa) from 1980 to 1985.
Professor at the UDK in Berlin since 2012.
Visiting professor at the TU in Berlin (2007-11), at the Peter Behrens School of architecture in Düsseldorf 2005, at the EPFL Lausanne in 2010-11. at the Pavillon Neuflize OBC-Palais de Tokyo, Paris, in 2013-2014.

PUBLICATIONS
Lacaton & Vassal 1993-2015, El Croquis n°177-178 Monograph, Spain, 2015
Lacaton & Vassal, 2G n°60 (2012), 2G Books (2010), 2G n°21 (2002) Monograph, editorial GG, Barcelona A+U, n°498 Monograph Japan, march 2012
DNK-110823 Lacaton&Vassal Editorial FRAC Nord-Pas de Calais, Dunkerque, France 2012
Druot, Lacaton&Vassal - Tour Bois Le Prêtre Editorial Ika & Andreas Ruby, Berlin, 2012
Lacaton & Vassal Editorial HYX, France, exhibition catalogue, Paris, 2009
PLUS - large scale housing development - An exceptional case Frédéric Druot, Anne Lacaton & Jean Philippe Vassal, Editorial GG, Barcelona, 2007

AWARDS
Simon Architecture Prize / Fondation Mies Van der Rohe - The Living Places with *Frédéric Druot and Christophe Hutin for the Transformation of 3 dwelling buildings*, Bordeaux, 2016
Life Time Achievement - Trienal de Arquitectura de Lisboa, 2016
Académie de l'Architecture, France - Gold Medal, 2016
Heinrich Tessenow - Gold Medal, Germany, 2016
Rolf Schock Prize, visual arts category, Sweden, 2014
Design of the year 2013, architecture category, England With *Frédéric Druot, architect, for the Transformation of the Housing block Tour Bois le prêtre*, Paris
Daylight & Building Components Award 2011, *Velux Foundation Copenhagen*
Grand Prix National d'Architecture 2008, France
International Fellow of Royal Institute of British Architects, 2009
Erich Schelling Award 2006 - *Fondation Erich Schelling*, Karlsruhe
Award "Sustainability and Residential Innovation", City of Madrid, 2006
Grand Prix National d'Architecture Jeune Talent, France, 1999
Lauréats des Albums de la Jeune Architecture, France, 1991
Mies Van der Rohe Award - European Prize for Contemporary Architecture
Final shortlist in 2007 for the Management Sciences University, Bordeaux, France
Final shortlist in 2003 for the Palais de Tokyo, Site for contemporary creation, Paris, France
Equerre d'Argent Award in 2011, France With *Frédéric Druot, architect, for the Transformation of the Housing block Tour Bois le prêtre*, Paris

Reinventing the world

In *Sense and non-sense* Maurice Merleau-Ponty suggests a rich reflection on the quest for reality by rereading the work of Cézanne: "The painter was only able to create an image. It took time for this image to come to life for others. In those times the work of art combined separate ways, there was no longer simply one like in a lasting dream or recurring nightmare, or in space like a coloured canvas, but it resided intact in several spirits, presumably every spirit possible, like something acquired forever"[1]. In other words, in *Cézanne's Doubt,* Maurice Merleau-Ponty points out an articulated process of interpretation of the reality contained in the work, which needs (and is consequently enriched by) a substantial feature of openness to interpretation on the part of those observing it. For Merleau-Ponty a painter like Cézanne, or an artist or philosopher, was not only able to create and express an idea but also to rekindle experiences that would root it in the minds of others. This interpretative frame suggests a reading of the reality of contexts that is open to different, changing interpretations also in other disciplines, like architecture; the way of thinking, designing and building the Lacaton & Vassal studio seems, in particular, to have pursued a similar search. Their works unfold in shapes and ramifications, just like a Cézanne painting, awaiting the observer's interpretation. The spatial reality of their houses cannot properly be understood except through free use by users. *To re-invent,* transform, add, overlay, re-use what exists for the pleasure of living, become the principles for rebuilding a relationship both between architecture and user, and between architecture and city. It is a case of a specific tendency in architectural research that is not representative but effectual to the substance and structurality of phenomena: the search for reality on the part of an architecture that cannot disregard the feature of openness to reading both by those who experience and use it, and on the part of those who, for the needs of planning, are led to interpret and reconstruct the reality proposed. "Its own relativisation – states Vittorio Gregotti – is moreover a deep aspect of design that comes from the best modernist tradition: that born, and which perpetually regenerates by means of its own critical attitude, namely the continuous debate on the conditions and actual cognition of reality, apart from its statutes". This taking of responsibility implies the loss of fixedness of contents and the opening to transformability, meant as adaptation to

[1]. Maurice Merleau-Ponty, *Senso e non senso,* Il Saggiatore Milan 2016, p. 38.

Massimo Faiferri

Palays de Tokyo, Paris

Reuse and transformation in Lacaton & Vassal's architecture

different contexts, both physical and cultural, delivering the project and its outcomes into the hands of the time that follows and different actors. So it is a question of the capacity of adaptation of architecture, obtained formulating a possibility principle, to which different ideas of form, use and place adapt: a relative dimension of design (open to possibilities) and not imperative (form and concluded space).

In *Opera aperta*[2], Umberto Eco targeted entirely new aesthetic horizons, handling the issue of works unrestricted by rigid structural and formal models; here the category *open* is used to define situations that are often different, but on the whole the types of work taken into consideration tend to single out a concept of work with a non-univocal outcome: "form is aesthetically valid to the extent to which it can be seen and understood from several perspectives, showing a richness of aspects and echoes without ever ceasing to be itself [...] In this sense, then, a work of art, complete, closed form in its perfection of perfectly calibrated organism, is also open, in the chance of being interpreted in a thousand different ways without its irreproducible uniqueness being changed. Each use is thus an interpretation and a performance, for in each use the work relives in an original perspective". This principle can be applied in architecture when a building, though marked by absolute geometry or finished form, leaves room for interpretation through its use. The configuration of the structural elements, the lay-out of the technological plant, the succession of spaces can guide and, in some cases, decidedly condition its use, the perception and thus actual interpretation of the work by the users.

In antiquity, too, formal alterations to an architectural building were used strategically to correct and guide specific perception of the building. Among the examples at the end of *Opera aperta*, Umberto Eco quotes the only case dealing with the architectural sphere in the book, namely Vitruvius and the concept of eurythmia as the adaptation of the objective proportions of the architectural building to the subjective requirements of the user's vision. "The various perspective artifices represent exactly that number of concessions made to the requirements of the observer's situation to lead him to see the figure in the only right way possible, that upon which the author (engineering visual artifices) tried to make the mind of the user converge" – the possibility is clear of configuring a building in such a way as to guide, if not determine, the degree of *openness* or *closure* of the relationship with the user, not just perception. As Eco specified later, open works also exist in a less metaphorical, more tangible sense, and he illustrated them with a series of other examples, to emphasise the possible degree of interpretation. In architecture it is a matter of the level of interpretation of the possibilities

---

[2]. Umberto Eco, *Opera aperta*, Bompiani, Milan 1962 Ed. 1.

for use, which some works are able to suggest to users via their inherent spatial and material configuration.

One of Lacaton & Vassal's projects that pursues this principle more than others is the transformation of the Palais de Tokyo in Paris into a contemporary art museum. Built in 1937 for the Exposition universelle, the Palais was then used as a national modern art gallery, a national centre of photography and cinema. In the 1990s it was abandoned to an indefinite destiny until the Ministry of Culture decided to use it, in 1999, as a space of creation and exhibition for contemporary artists. In the meantime, the interior had been altered considerably, with terrible deterioration due to the succession of different uses that had made the configuration and spatial complexity of the building almost unrecognisable. In Lacaton & Vassal's proposal to restore it a transformation strategy emerged that made good use of the physical and aesthetic feature of the complex, with minimal transformations to improve accessibility and safety. The Palais de Tokyo therefore became a changing, fluid space with no subdivisions, to promote multiple use of the spaces. This is a significant work indeed for its degree of indefiniteness and openness: architecture that organises a weave of communicative effects such that any user may understand its transformation and original form. Reacting to the weave of stimuli proposed, the user takes with him, however, a concrete existential situation, his individual sensitivity and specific culture, together with personal tastes, inclinations and prejudices; understanding the original form thus takes place along a series of perspectives, showing itself with a wealth of echoes, but never preventing the building from being itself. Not by chance, the works and art installations exhibited amplify these echoes, multiplying the interpretations of spaces and their features. The 8,000 sq.m of the first phase of the works were inaugurated in 2001 with enormous success: the Palais de Tokyo's bare spaces, devoid of trimmings, fully ready for the changing requirements of exhibitions, became an indispensable worldwide reference point for contemporary art lovers. In 2012, with the second phase of the works, the area of intervention expanded by a further 14,000 sq.m; the plan was completed with film projection rooms, concerts halls, open cafés on the terrace, a bookshop-shop and an administration area. The complex play of spaces at different levels of the original building finally became visible in its entirety, thanks also to new distribution centres, created to facilitate access to the four floors of the building and have it conform with fire regulations. The project's basic principle is linked with creating a hierarchy of areas to optimise the spaces, due to the removal of superfluous components, and to creating environments able to accommodate simultaneous events, without interference.

The configuration of the Palais of Tokyo was approached by the critics[3] at one of the most fascinating projects of the 1960s. With it Cedric Price

FRAC Nord Pas de calais

proposed a new concept of architecture opposing the axioms of the modern movement: his Fun Palace of 1961 was in fact an interactive construction, able to be configured by users. By moving the mobile elements, visitors could become an active part of the compositional process, giving life to scenes that could be continually reprogrammed. The Fun Palace model is very simple: a rectangular building, dotted with fifteen metallic towers, intended to support the secondary structures as well as contain plant and service elements. The cranes to be used to move, from one part to another, the materials necessary for configuring the interior were placed on the top of the towers, contributing to defining a construction without a plan, that develops with an interactive process based on the variation and changing nature of the requirements. Though far from utopian inspiration, the Palais de Tokyo project seems to follow the track marked out by Price's Fun Palace, also followed, moreover, by other experiments, such as the radical visions of Archigram and Yona Friedman or Renzo Piano and Richard Rogers' design for the Centre Pompidou nearby.

In short, it is an idea of construction without a specific manifesto, able to change its plan from time to time and appear as an ever new, different spatial event: Lacaton & Vassal's architectures consider the project's positive virtue to be the *readiness* of the work to be interpreted, used and configured in different ways. "To write means to make the meaning of the world waver – Roland Barthes[4] wrote –, to place an indirect query on it to which the writer, due to last-minute indecision, refrains from responding. The answer is given by each of us, bringing his history, his language, his freedom, but since history, language and freedom change endlessly, the response of the world of the writer is endless"; similarly, Lacaton & Vassal refer to those using their buildings for the response.

From user to inhabitant

The fifth chapter of *Lessons for Students in architecture*[5], one of the most interesting texts on teaching architecture that appeared at the end of the last century, is entitled *From User to Dweller*: Herman Hertzberger develops the concept by exploring some of its schools, mostly earmarked for Montessori

[3]. Gonzalo Herrero Delicado and Maria José Marcos, *Il Fun Palace contemporaneo*, in "Domus", 2012, June, 959, p. 42.
[4]. Roland Barthes, in the *Avant-propos de Sur Racine*, Paris 1963: "Écrire, c'est ébranler le sens du monde, y disposer une interrogation indirecte, à laquelle l'écrivain, par un dernier suspens, s'abstient de répondre. La réponse, c'est chacun de nous qui la donne, y apportant son histoire, son langage, sa liberté ; mais comme histoire, langage et liberté changent infiniment, la réponse du monde à l'écrivain est infinie".
[5]. Herman Hertzberger, *Lessons for Students in Architecture*, 010, Rotterdam 1991, It. trad. *Lezioni di Architettura*, Laterza, Bari 1996, p. 21.

Schools. His thought goes beyond the themes linked with education, to define the universal aspects that every architectural project has to address, in the sense of design for the space for the life of man in democratic societies: "In organising the plan of a building, at the moment when plan and section are designed and also on the basis of the principle of installations, the conditions can be created for a greater sense of responsibility and consequently also greater involvement in the lay-out and furnishing of an area. Only then do the users become inhabitants".

The first of the buildings chosen by Hertzberger to illustrate the theme was the Delft Montessori School (1960-66). In this building the Dutch architect tries to give shape and life to a sort of urban landscape where the classrooms are metaphorically houses, placed along a street, represented by the common spaces of the school; the teachers, together with the children, are entrusted with the task of defining the atmosphere of the interior of the houses/classrooms. In configuring the spaces, the school manages to express educational principles based on carrying out domestic duties inside the school building, with the objective of strengthening the children's emotional affinity with the context. By keeping their own house/classroom tidy, the child builds up an affective link with the environment he frequents every day; with elements of everyday home life (like green plants, placed in suitable niches) and exposure to manual activities (displayed in showcases), the pupils make the school environments homely, becoming an active part of the construction of environments where they identify themselves as members of a community.

In various other projects Hertzberger has structured flexible, modifiable environments depending on the uses and features the individual user wishes to organise within them. Pursuing this objective, architecture manages on the one hand to represent the space of experience, necessary to develop learning, and on the other tries to encourage a process of identification/appropriation by the inhabitants. The more influence you can personally have on the things that surround you – Hertzberger wrote in 1967[6]–, the more emotionally involved you will feel and the more attention you will give them, and you will also be more ready to lavish love and care on the things around you. We can develop affection only for those things to which we belong, things onto which we can project so much of our identity and in which we can invest so much care and devotion that they become a part of us.

In other words, any user of architecture manages to interpret the role of *inhabitant* only if they feel themselves involved in the definition of spaces and forms of the built environment, in a continuous cross-referencing between the parts, founded on the reciprocity of roles: user and form strengthen each other and interact in a similar relationship to that between individual and

[6]. Herman Hertzberger, *Identity*, in "Forum", 1967, 7.

community. The spaces of buildings, especially in the school environment, should therefore be imagined as *places,* in which the individuals can recognise themselves as active parts of a collectivity: spaces that change, precursors of a kind of urbanity as complex as it is open to social aggregation phenomena. Recent studies by Marco Iacoboni[7], a scientist known for his research on Giacomo Rizzolatti's mirror neurons, have proved that human biology predisposed individuals to empathy. Empathy and its consequences are not mechanical processes but are filtered by culture and cultural types and specificities, causing different kinds of perception and reaction compared with pure sensorial stimuli. Cultural and emotional affinities favour and facilitate the empathy process, intensifying its efficacy. Iacoboni's studies are a further confirmation of the essential, irreplaceable function of a building that is conceived as a *common place,* where different generations and various forms of life, thought and culture may confront each other and enter into dialogue. From this point of view Lacaton & Vassal's design for the Nantes school of architecture appears significant: a large structure of some 25,000 sq.m on three different levels. The building is characterised by a simple construction system consisting of a light structure in steel and reinforced concrete; the rationality of the structural grid, together with the service blocks and ascending elements, permits a variety of internal configurations, preparing the building in advance for adaptations and alterations, as well as future expansion. The programme spaces are assigned to large volumes with double height, with their functions not defined; they may be used by students, professors and external individuals for initiatives. An authentic *open* structure, in Eco's sense of the word, able to generate and favour new relations with the user: formalism has to give way to the capacity to think of complex functioning, due to the relationship between man and building. A ramp gives energy to the building and links the three levels with the city, creating a series of rich, diversified situations. By energising the space and introducing the concepts of ambulatory and peripatetic space, to be experienced through the senses, the project recalls the phenomenological concept of space based on movement, as found – for example – in some of Steven Holl's works. The great openings of perspectives project the line of vision outside and, at the same time, englobe the landscape within the school rooms, enriching further the users' perceptive experience.

For Lacaton & Vassal structural freedom is fundamental and indispensable for their way of conceiving architecture; it is pursued in all their works by means of a grid independent from its content, so that it is the content that emerges and defines the features of the space. On occasions when they

---

[7]. Marco Iacoboni, *I neuroni specchio. Come capiamo ciò che fanno gli altri*, Bollati Boringhieri, Turin 2008.

address pre-existing elements, too, Lacaton & Vassal nevertheless seek a harmonious relationship between the existing and the new. Their numerous renovation projects bear their signature in terms of a synthesis between present structures and structures necessary for alterations, while new-build projects show a synthesis between programmatic situations underlying the project and possible developments of subsequent options. The overlapping of two structures (through their relations, differences and at the same time affinities) promotes the development of unforeseen phenomena, with the unexpected use of the environments and unusual behaviour models of users. This synthesis may materialise in projects that express faith in the future, through a desired lack of definition of the spaces and uses.

In transforming the Tour Bois-le-Prêtre building in Paris the overlapping of new and old is explicitly seen: the renovation has radically changed the image of the tower but the layers composing it can easily be identified. In the old building the furniture tells of a pre-existing layer that has endured and is amplified in a new idea for living proposed by the extension. The external winter garden does not propose a new function so much as improve the quality of the apartments in terms of space, comfort and microclimate. The radical change in the living conditions enables the view over the surrounding landscape to be enjoyed and different air breathed also inside the old building, breaking the physical boundaries of the building and mental ones of the inhabitants. It is all this that makes Lacaton & Vassal's extensions so surprising.

This process was clearly recounted by the exhibition on the Tour Bois-le-Prêtre project, installed in 2012 by the DAM Museum in Frankfurt. The exhibition was curated by Ilka and Andreas Ruby in collaboration with the Something Fantastic studio and displayed real images of the apartment interiors, concerning above all the extension, including the winter gardens and open balconies: a sort of frieze containing the pictures ran uninterruptedly along the walls for 50 m on the top floor of the DAM. The exhibition was completed with furniture, plants and other elements, placed opposite the pictures, so that visitors felt as though they were inside one of the apartments, experiencing the everyday life of the Tour Bois-le-Prêtre tenants, with an exceptional view of Paris on the horizon. Forgetting the museum, one could comfortably discover from one of the exhibition seats, armchairs or sofas how each apartment had been freely interpreted by the single owners; the visitor became in turn a user and, to a certain extent, took part in the process of interpretation of the tower as apartments.

The story of this and other similar experiences has been the subject of various other exhibitions; some were organised in recent years by our research group, as part of several occasions in collaboration with Lacaton & Vassal, also in the teaching field[8]. Organising these exhibitions was also a

Tour Bois le Pretre, Paris

pretext for studying further their approach to the transformation of existing architecture: for Lacaton & Vassal it is an opportunity to develop the process they call *re-invention*. The contemporary city offers many situations able to stimulate this approach; to grasp the opportunity however, the situation has to be carefully observed close up, so as to understand the true potential of transforming existing buildings, with the purpose of proposing a transformation endowed with both a greater level of comfort and quality, and a better relationship with the climate and environment.

Space and structure

A series of theoretical reflections that developed from the 1950s onwards, when structuralism and semiology began to be widely studied, suggested the possibility that architects may also create a *structure*, in the sense specified by Barthes for writers and artists. This approach was a fascinating factor for some research work on the analogy between architecture and linguistic structure by a group of Dutch architects, whose work was published by the review "Forum"; among them, it was Herman Hertzberger who pointed out the need to reconsider forms of architecture, which he considered to be cold and lifeless, repressive rather than liberating. A theorist of open form, as we have said, Hertzberger always sought stable configurations, permanent and recognisable, but at the same time sufficiently modifiable as to enable each individual to express his aesthetic and functional preferences, making the improvements he considered necessary. To describe this principle, Hertzerger suggested the comparison between the relationship of architectural forms with their readiness for individual interpretation and that of language with the word. His model was based on the existence of a fundamental *objective structure* of forms: a sequence of socially legitimised configurations, within which the architect could not create anything completely new but had to limit himself to objects able to be reconsidered by users for the purpose of realising new, unexpected situations. The architect cannot be harassed by the need for total control but has to be abled to organise structures: from aesthete of the absolute the designer turns into organiser of what is possible. Hertzberger's projects for school buildings are the most significant example of this. In the search for a system able to make the world intelligible, to reconstitute it in architectural form, this impulse proved to be one of the main worries of the architecture of the end of the sixties/seventies of the last century.

---

[8]. See, among others, the exhibitions organised by the research lab *ecourbanlab* at the DADU, Alghero, Scientific Supervisor Massimo Faiferri: *Re-invent, Lacaton &Vassal*, il Ghetto, Cagliari, 1-17 April 2016, and Torre San Giovanni, Alghero, 3-14 June 2014.

The works presented here show some affinity with similar research. Lacaton & Vassal's inclination for permitting users greater articulation of spaces has been discussed; the many opportunities for internal organisation offered by the structured grid proposed as an essential principle of their way of designing, express a fundamental principle of freedom. Guaranteed by the structure, this freedom of movement, of different activity, of resting or contemplation, enables numerous ways to unfold of appropriating space. At this point it should be specified that the term *structure* can have at least three different meanings in architecture, referring respectively to: the building in its entirety; the system of support of a building; the model by which a project, building or city becomes intelligible. In Lacaton & Vassal's case the term *structure* may be useful to develop a reflection halfway between the second and third meanings.

Structure, as a specific element (fully linked with the means of support), is characterised in Lacaton & Vassal's works by light construction systems with a framework, typically featuring independence from a plan and a delicate impact, as well by the wide span size. The greater, wider and more spacious the structure, the greater the number of stories that will be able to unfold within the building. From this point of view, Lacaton & Vassal refer explicitly to the Maison Dom-Ino model and seem to pursue the expressive tradition of the skeleton structure in Dutch architecture, which began its development with the Zonnestraal of Hilversum, realised in 1926 by Johannes Duiker, taken up again by Hertzberger (with the extension to the Amsterdam Sloterdijk industrial laundry in 1964) and continued in subsequent works, via a combination of the anthropological visions of Van Eyck with a structural-rationalist tendency inherited from Berlage. If, on the other hand, Lacaton & Vassal's works are observed through an analysis of the structure as a means to achieve intelligibility, it is unlikely that an ambiguous overlap with the first meaning of structure will slip through. On one hand, the physical structure of the support elements present is clearly perceptible in a large number of the projects, especially in the case of extensions, while on the other, the conceptual project structure cannot be clear but through the physical choice of the supporting grid. The second and third meanings of structure are actually strongly linked for Lacaton & Vassal: the second is only a particular case of the third. In the works presented in this book, the structure is an indispensable metaphor for the development of the project or, rather, it can represent two different metaphors, coming from different fields.

School of architecture, Nantes

Less is more

Even the most distracted gaze will not miss the simplicity of the constructive systems and the elementary nature of the geometries adopted by Lacaton & Vassal. The constructive rationality of the structural elements is characteristic of their works, which have the further objective of determining a new relationship with the climate and environment. By supplying favourable conditions for changing administration of the spaces, their works are able to encroach upon what exists and generate new urban conditions inside the buildings.

This attitude towards construction is expressed in the use of technologies and sustainable materials that are simple and economic, revealing an ethical approach to the profession of architect that surpasses the need to give immediate answers to requirements and expectations of those inhabiting their buildings. Lacaton & Vassal's constructive details do not dominate the design scene: in placing themselves at the service of science and technology rather than aesthetics, the joints, slots and finishings try above all to clarify the structure in its entirety. Space is the undisputed master of the project, simple, essential space, like the structure that determines it and accompanies it in its definition: space potentially open to the variety of uses that the user will wish to define.

From this point of view, Lacaton & Vassal's works may be compared with the work of Glenn Murcutt and his "rough and refined"[9] architecture, observant of the climatic conditions of Australia, but also flexible and adaptable over time. Most of Murcutt's domestic interiors, like those of Lacaton & Vassal, are narrowed down to the definition of the sense of places, in an intense relationship with the environment; they have a particular conception of domestic space in common, where the landscape becomes a scenario. In many of Murcutt's projects the external world is *measured,* taking it back to normal, that is controllable, dimensions; as they open up towards the endless stretch of the Australian landscapes, his houses refuse the idea of domesticity as renunciation, embodying instead the idea of *open refuge.* Similarly, Lacaton & Vassal's projects to transform residential buildings propose new domesticity by breaking down the perimeter walls of the existing building and setting up new open spaces, facing the outside. Just as Murcutt's houses may be defined *revelatory machines* of the extraordinary environment surrounding them, Lacaton & Vassal's interiors also *reveal* and englobe the unexpressed potential of the peripheral landscapes in which they are set. The architectural strategies adopted – like passive cooling systems and the various paraments for protection from the sun – become instruments of manipulation of light

---

[9]. Massimo Faiferri, *Un'architettura rude e raffinata: opere recenti di Glenn Murcutt,* in "Area", 2009, 107, pp. 4-15.

and space, machines with a simple tactile and visual presence that open (and close where necessary) but also enrich, with their variations, the spatial experience of the inhabitant. The rough elegance of Murcutt's buildings is largely the result of the wise use of simple constructive systems and their novel assembly in solutions of extraordinary elegance. Similarly, Lacaton & Vassal propose *rough* architectures by using common materials, easy to obtain, which in their immediate materiality are, however, recomposed with constructive *elegance*.

In this sense, Lacaton & Vassal constitute a model, to be carefully observed, particularly in periods of economic crisis, during which the work of those following alternative routes than mere research for formal results, takes on even more value and interest. The philosophy underlying their work is: to gain the *maximum possible,* in order to obtain liveable space with the least expense, in a sort of *less is more* of Miesian memory, but going beyond the ideological, figurative aspects typical of the expert's works to concentrate mainly on the essentiality of the project and economy of buildings. To achieve this objective Lacaton & Vassal borrow construction techniques from the industrial and agricultural landscapes, in some ways elementary, but with great potential, including figurative. A sort of manifesto of these principles is represented by Maison Latapie in Floirac, built in 1993 in the suburbs of Bordeaux, from which a series of variants ensued in subsequent projects. A characteristic of the housing is a double skin: the external one in galvanised metal and polycarbonate, translucid and ventilated, contains another one, made of an opaque volume; the declared objective is to add further space to the house, on the same budget. Half the volume is an area that, oscillating between inside and out, may be experienced in different ways, depending on the requirements and the season. Lacaton & Vassal manage to create a *fluid* space, made available for different uses, without resorting to complex technologies, but simply using *rough* elements, of an industrial nature; the *elegance* of their assembly defines spaces with great charm and personality, which bring to mind Murcutt's architectures.

The evolution of this research continued with a project for Mulhouse, when Jean Nouvel, entrusted with drawing up the *masterplan* of an area of the city, called for some architecture studies for social housing. Contrary to what almost all the participants proposed, Lacaton & Vassal designed a building with 14 duplex apartments in which the prevailing formal element was a zinc-coated industrial structure, lined with polycarbonate: a conservatory through and through, including in its geometry, characterised by the classic lowered arch roof. Apart from being very economic, this construction technique permits large openings and, inside, a free space with very few dividing elements; compared with the housing of the other designers who participated, those of Lacaton & Vassal were much larger, with a decidedly lower construction cost. The message this building carries, a constant one in all their subsequent work, is that true luxury is the quantity of space made available – the objective underlying every Lacaton & Vassal project from then on would be the achievement of the maximum space possible with the budget available.

Etihcs and aesthetics

Lacaton & Vassal's projects to be seen in these pages remind us how the suburbs of contemporary metropolises, being representative of hardship and of social emergency but also, to a certain degree, of an aesthetic of inhabiting, make clear the need to counteract the ordinariness of the highly diversified planning strategies based on the acknowledgement of ramification and differentiation of the concept of cultural, economic, social and figurative progress. It is a state of the problem (with complex aspects - compositional and multiform - still neglected by contemporary planners) that shares the same principles of exclusion at the base of the origin of the contemporary metropolis. As Yona Friedman suggests, this controversial aspect may prove to be surprisingly creative: in *L'Architecture de survie. Une philosopie de la pauvreté*[10] Friedman clarifies very well some points of this reflection. In the chapter *La pauvreté neuve* he explains that the "new poor" are of two types: those who tend to belong to the Western world, the industrialised countries (they are those who earn money but do not have enough either to get a home and food, or to satisfy norms and conventions of the times); those who, in non-industrialised countries leave the countryside with the illusion of improving their living conditions in the city (and thus the *bidonville* phenomenon materialises in third world metropolises). They have a problem in common, Friedman states: how to guarantee their survival? A reflection on the theme of *residence* is needed, its configurations and features, including figurative ones, to extend the concept of *emergency* also to those pockets of hardship that are present even in the better developed countries. Beauty has always been a part of man's needs, representing - in every epoch and the various cultures - an apparently useless, superfluous *quid,* which expresses the true need for things. Objects for common use represent something more than their simple use, just as houses or cities aspire to something more than being a simple functional response to settlement needs. The *not beautiful* of contemporary life has urged many layers of society to act in an ecological vein; the widespread sensation of impoverishment of the environmental resources, combined with worry over the spoiling of landscapes, worsened

---

[10]. Published in the first French edition in 1978 and translated into Italian by Bollati Boringhieri in 2009 as *L'architettura di sopravvivenza. Una filosofia della povertà.*

by the destruction of ecosystems, has caused environmental movements to spread and they have obtained greater attention to these aspects in public opinion. Unfortunately, the declared objective of these movements has not always been an encounter with the beautiful and the sustainable of the ecological initiatives; many battles fought under the ecologist's flag have concealed dubious morals with unstated aims.

For a definition of modern *venustas,* attention must be paid to the ethical implications of *sustainable construction,* meant in the widest sense possible. Lacaton & Vassal's projects propose a search for beauty to a reasonable degree, renunciation, moderation and careful management of resources, but also of ecological and cultural variety, special features and local identity rediscovered. In the cultural context of contemporary times ethics seems mainly an alternative to aesthetics, while the interpretative models and instruments developed to draw close to the beautiful have not been able to contribute to giving it an exhaustive definition; perhaps coupling the concept of beautiful in architecture with an ethics of the project aimed at satisfying evident (but ignored) needs and requirements, might be a departure point to make *venustas* topical.

Architecture may dress up civic values, to the extent to which it is considered an urban and community asset, regardless of designers or clients: should architectural planning not perhaps respond to the need (this, too, in other times, belonging to ethical components) to create constructions practical to use, easy to build, with realistic costs and high aesthetic quality? Or is aesthetic quality an added value, which belongs only to some kinds of architecture, often of the figurative self-congratulatory type, and is reserved for a few lucky users. Perhaps it will indeed be the role of the ethics of *good construction* to discriminate between good and bad architecture, freeing us from many stereotypes: in this light, the works of Lacaton & Vassal seem to propose a sort of aesthetics of necessity, pursuing these principles quietly, with simplicity, courtesy and elegance, and no ideological weight.

Modification and transformation

One of the themes for which Lacaton & Vassal are known throughout the world is the encounter with the building patrimony that is the fruit of rationalism, which gave itself the praiseworthy objective of creating social housing, in a short time and at low cost, thus becoming typical of the European suburbs of Europe. The Paris *banlieue* was also dotted over time with the *grands ensembles* of social housing: the Tour Bois-le-Prêtre was one of these cases, a horrible 16-floor building in Paris's *17° arrondissement* which, in 2005, was the subject of a competition for renovation, as has been seen.

Housing trasformation, San Nazaire

Lacaton & Vassal's winning project, together with Frédéric Druot, proposed a new envelope for the old building, with a planned budget of 40% less compared with the demolition and reconstruction of the tower. Apart from defining a new exterior, the operation had as its objectives both an increase in the areas of the apartments and improved spatial and functional quality, together with reduced heat dispersion: in place of the small windows, wide, transparent openings, changing the image of the tower and improving quality and comfort within. The crucial aspect of the project was the relationship with the inhabitants, who stayed in their houses for almost the whole duration of the works, going away only for a few days. The project could have been limited to small modifications, promptly acting on a few terraces and simply making the whole more attractive; actually, the project only had one true objective: to offer the inhabitants the opportunity to improve their living conditions. As for other projects shown in these pages, the facades of the Tour Bois-le-Prêtre are examples that demonstrate how it is possible to give back dignity to modest buildings, weighing as little as possible on the environment and the economy, through little but significant transformation work, able to give back a space with high quality.

Planners need to find new interpretative keys of reality, conceiving architecture as a specific form of knowledge, a way to understand and interpret the world; architecture, as a cognitive activity, according to Monestiroli[11] rises from a dual dialectical relationship: on the one hand, with the social and material reality belonging to each epoch, openly confronting the various needs, new materials and new technologies – innovation; on the other, with the historic reality of architecture as a discipline – tradition. For as much as architecture belongs to the realm of ideas, it is nurtured and draws its energy from the reality it interprets and to which it is ultimately answerable; the true task of the architect consists indeed of interpreting reality, structuring it with the intervention of thought and trying to make it intelligible, namely endowing it with architecture.

To understand the city and work there, one needs to consider it a concatenation of objects, made and desired by man, which altogether form a fabric of places, in their turn made up of buildings, roads and parks. "To mould our cities and make them an expression of us – Rykwert explains – the constant participation of the community is indispensable, its constant involvement, an idea that seems to have been tragically forgotten by the various bodies that govern us. To understand the city in its dynamic three-dimensional aspects, to follow and modulate its self-generation process, connect and extend its fabric, a study of man is necessary; there is the need to under-

---

[11]. Antonio Monestiroli, *L'architettura della realtà*, Allemandi, Turin 2004, p. 14.
[12]. Joseph Rykwert, *La seduzione del luogo*, Einaudi, Turin 2003, p. 307.

stand how human experience transforms the built form into images"[12]. In the construction of the "new urban landscapes" of contemporary times, these aspects need a complex planning process, devoid of consolidated rules, open to fortuitous trends and able to include them in a new heterogeneous group: a design process like that proposed by Lacaton & Vassal, in which the conditions the designer finds, and transformations he determines, are made to converge. "In particular, the operation of synthesising the past and one's own epoch – Rogers wrote – characterised the creation of phenomena since, basically, it gave different meanings to the notion of tradition. One might say, indeed, that the creative process (namely the essential value of tradition that is dynamic and evolutive) depended on the different degree to which past and present took part in the 'becoming' of history, and this occurred regardless of scientific knowledge of past history or the programmatic awareness of the present"[13].

From this point of view, the concept of transformation takes on a significant role in planning dynamics. To speak of transformation implies acknowledging that there is always something pre-existing from which to start, something that, even when transformed, will conserve some constant features, elements of continuity. It is a view of being architects and urbanists that can be found in a nutshell in a fundamental passage from *La centina e l'arco* by Carlos Martí Arís: "Through the concept of transformation, understood as an intellectual operation, contemporary architecture can reconstitute its ties with tradition. Thus, the subject of transformation is not just a building, not something material but rather, the relations, the grammar rules that govern or support a structure"[14].

To *Reinvent the world* for Lacaton & Vassal means to start always from what exists, subjecting it to variations, developments and transgressions. Following this manipulation, from working with the forms, a new, different global form will arise: the project, which may be understood as the passage from one form to another, in search of a fusion of "the linguistic registers of the pre-existing, of the new, and their connection"[15]. In Lacaton & Vassal's works the theme of re-use, or rather of re-invention, becomes planning's main guide, trying to overlap pre-existing systems with new intentions (without imposing them) and seeking a fair balance between past and future, convinced that the well-being, dreams and hopes of contemporary society will be able to be pursued following these principles.

---

[13]. Ernesto Nathan Rogers, *Gli elementi del fenomeno architettonico*, Guida, Naples 1990, p. 92.
[14]. Carlos Martí Arís, *La centina e l'arco*, Marinotti, Milan 2007, p. 45.
[15]. Franco Purini, *Comporre l'architettura*, Laterza, Bari 2000, p. 51.

Tour Bois le Pretre, Paris

HOUSE
CAP FERRET

Exposed to the southeast and long unoccupied, the terrain is one of the last remaining non-built plots on the immediate shoreline of Arcachon Bay. A stretch of sand dune covered with arbutuses, mimosas and 46 pine trees rises then rapidly descends once more towards the Bay.

How does one preserve the dune and its vegetation, when building round and about means to cut down trees and even to build right on the ground? To avoid the felling of pine trees and the clearing of the low vegetation of the arbutuses, whose impact, seen from the Bay, is particularly perceptible. To raise the house above the ground in order to profit from the view.

To exclude the heavy earthworks which are particularly degrading for a ground surface of sand, twelve micro-piles are driven eight to ten meters deep. On top a metal frame, which creeps up between the trees, has been assembled.

The facade on the Bay side is open and glazed; the three others are more closed and intersected with transparent bays.

The height beneath the platform is variable, but always sufficient to permit one to pass under it. Like the side facades, the underside consists of aluminium panels, creating an artificial sky which, because the undulations are perpendicular to the Bay, reflects its luminosity.

The pine trees are preserved, including those situated within the four walls of the building itself. These trees traverse the house in special holders adapted to their swaying, their growth and their maintenance in a good state of health.

Running along the edge of the beach, the traditional wooden retaining wall has been remade.

location
Cap Ferret, France
year
1998
type
habitat housing
client
private
status
built
size
180 m^2 + 30 m^2 terrace
cost
123 000 € HT/net (val. 1998)
architects
Anne Lacaton & Jean Philippe Vassal
architects collaborators
Sylvain Menaud, Laurie Baggett, Emmanuelle Delage, Christophe Hutin, Pierre Yves Portier, David Pradel
phytosanitation consultant
Cesma, Ingerop, engineers, INRA, wood rheology, Mr

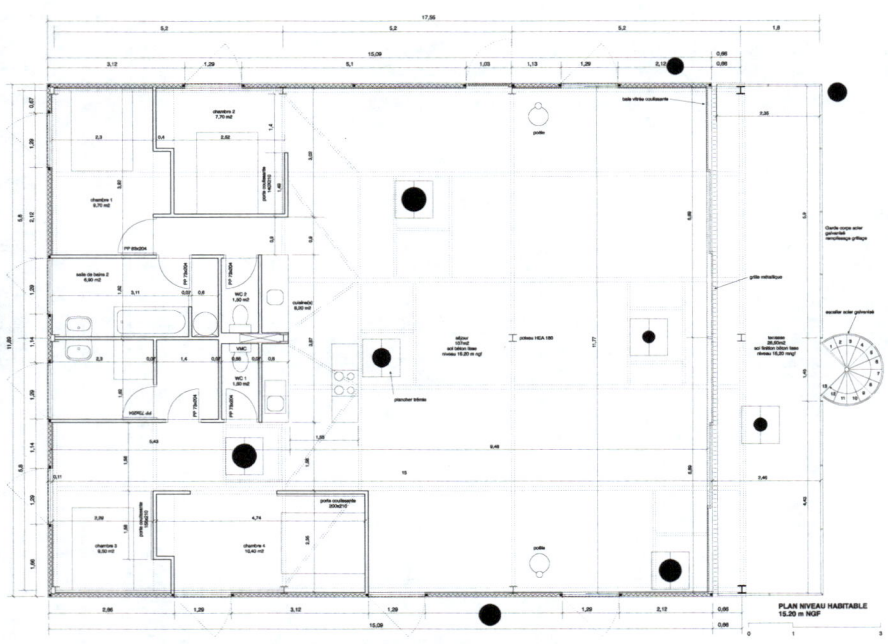

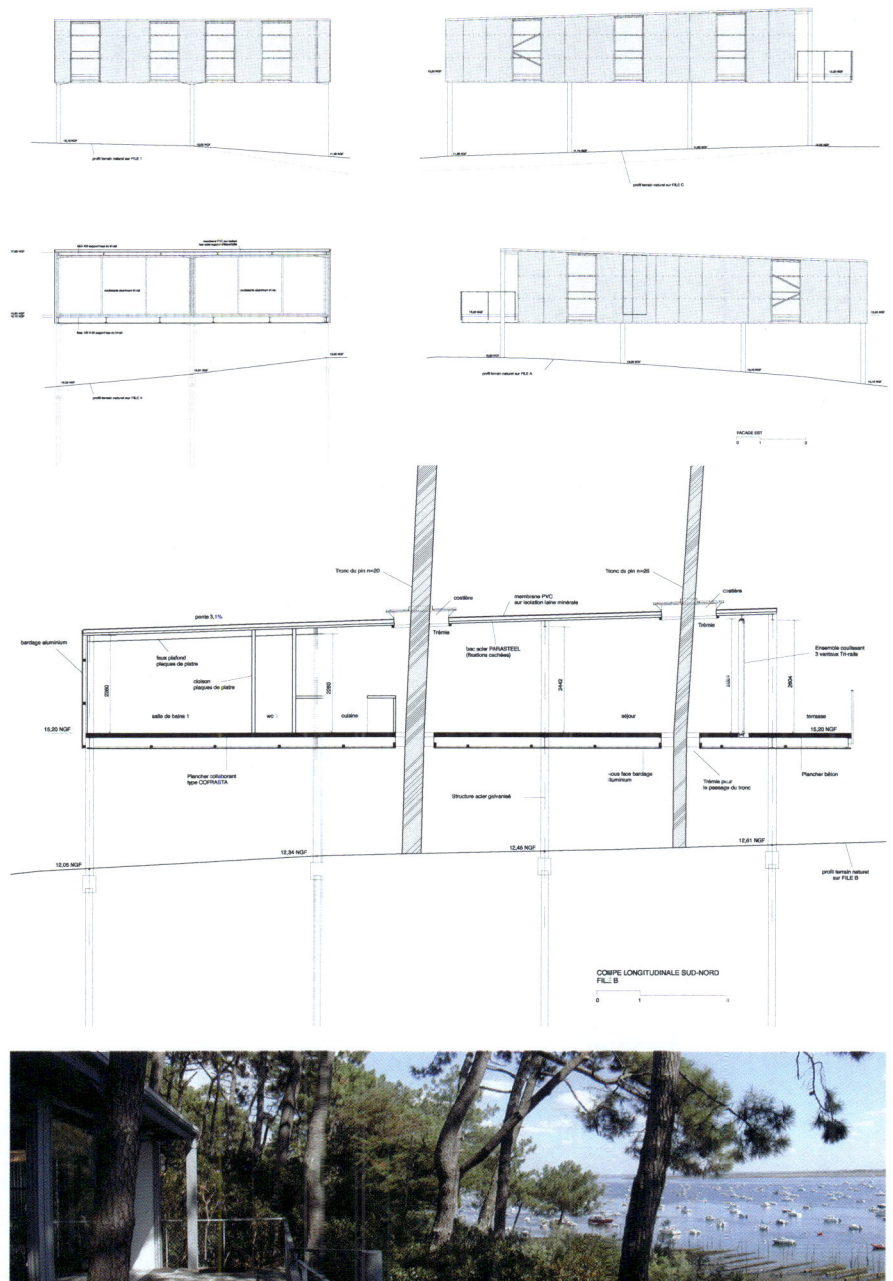

Reuse and transformation in Lacaton & Vassal's architecture

LATAPIE HOUSE

The inexpensive house is the result of a commission to build, on a low budget, a house for a couple with two children.
Located in a discontinuous residential area, the house fits into the street profile. It's a simple volume on a rectangular base that posits two open platforms. On a metal frame, one half, on the street side, is covered with opaque fiber-cement sheeting, and the other half, on the garden side, with transparent polycarbonate sheeting, forming a conservatory.
A wooden volume, clamped into the frame behind the opaque sheeting, defines an insulated and heated winter space opening onto the conservatory and the street-side exterior. The conservatory faces east and gets the early morning sun. It's an inhabitable part of the house, equipped with ample ventilation panels for comfort in summer.
The mobile nature of the east and west facades enables the house to change from its most closed to its most open state according to the need and desire for light, transparency, intimacy, protection and ventilation.
The inhabitable part of the house can vary according to the seasons, from the smallest (living room and bedrooms) to the largest area, by integrating the entire garden in high summer.

location
Floirac, France
year
1993
type
habitat housing
client
private
status
built
size
185 m^2
cost
55 275 € HT/net (val. 1993)
architects
Anne Lacaton & Jean-Philippe Vassal
architect collaborator
Sylvain Menaud
engineering
CESMA (metal structure),
Ingérop Sud Ouest (foundation)

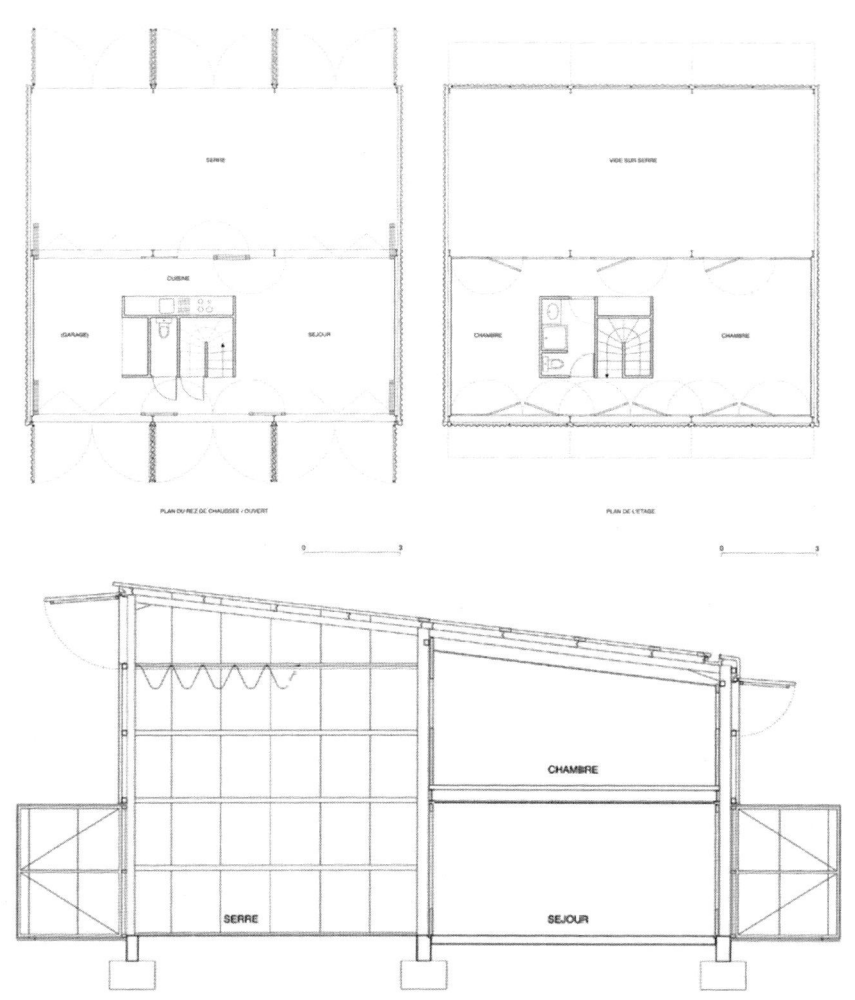

Reuse and transformation in Lacaton & Vassal's architecture

TRANSFORMATION OF HOUSING BLOCK TOUR BOIS LE PRÊTRE

Built in the early sixties along the ring road of Paris, this high rise block of 16 storeys includes 96 apartments. The demolition, firstly envisaged, has been avoided and a project of transformation decided. The project propose a generous extension of the apartments.

New floors, built as a self-supporting structure, are added on the periphery of the existing building at every floor, to extend the living rooms, create closeable terrasses and balconies. The existing facades with small windows will be removed and replaced by large transparent openings, so that the inhabitants will profit of the exceptionnal view on Paris all around.

Groundfloor the entrance hall will be refurbished. The floor will be made on a level with the exterior.

The volume will be releases of all useless rooms and installations to become a free and transparent space from the entrance to a new garden created on the back of the building.

Rooms for collective activities will be etablished on the sides of the hall. Two lifts will be built to improve the access to the apartments. The structure will be designed with prefabricated elements so that the inhabitants can stay in the apartments during the construction works.

location
Paris, France
year
2011
type
transformation
client
Paris Habitat
status
built
size
8900 m^2 existing + 3560 m^2 extension
cost
11,25 M€ HT/net
architects
Frédéric Druot, Anne Lacaton & Jean-Philippe Vassal
architects collaborators
Adis Tatarévic, Florian de Pous, Miho Nagashima, Caroline Stahl, Mario Bonilla, David Pradel
structure
VP & Green engineers
engineers systems
Inex
cost estimate
E.2.1
acoustics
Jourdan
fire security consultant
Vulcanéo

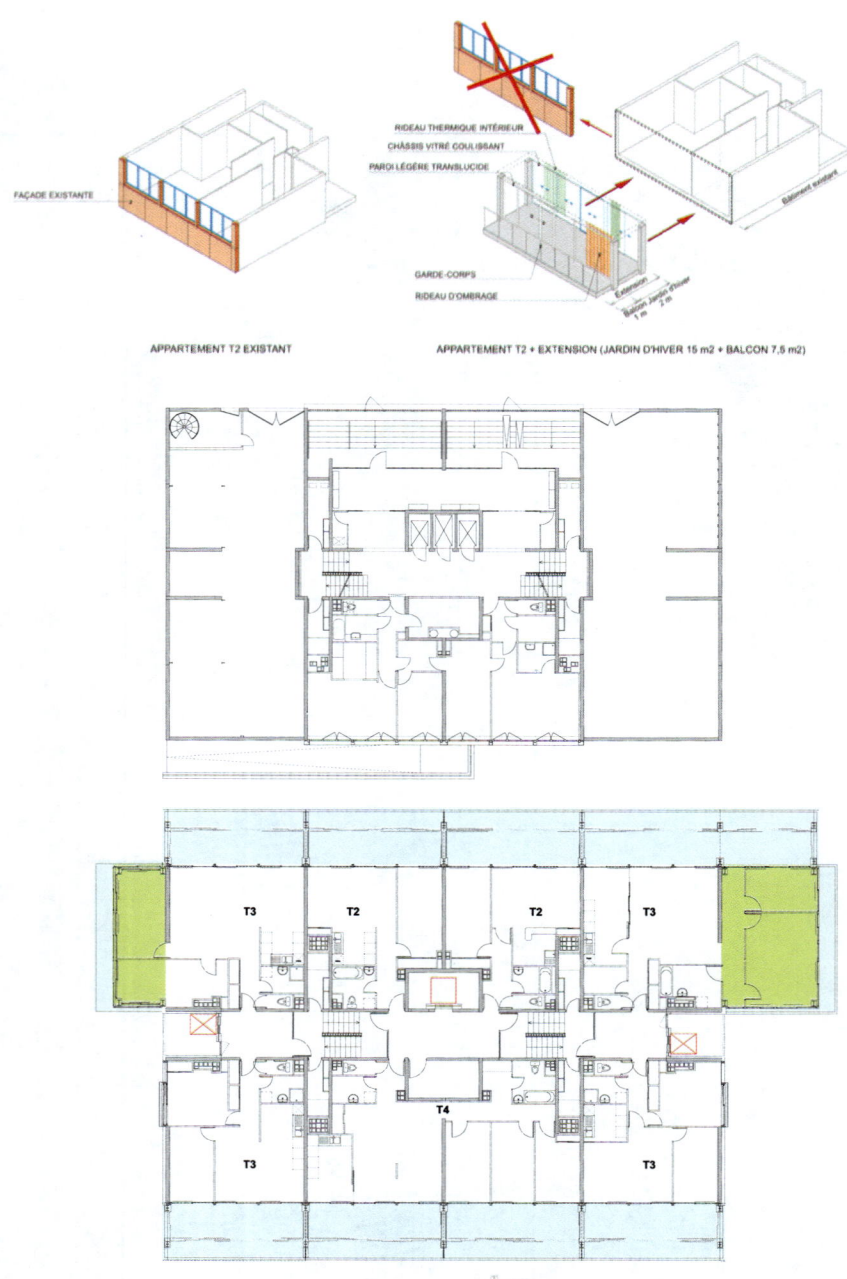

Reuse and transformation in Lacaton & Vassal's architecture

Reuse and transformation in Lacaton & Vassal's architecture

TRANSFORMATION OF 530 DWELLINGS BORDEAUX

The project consists in the transformation of 3 modernist social housing's buildings, fully occupied. It is part of the renovation program of the 'Cité du Grand Parc' in Bordeaux.

Built from the early 60's, this modernist district counts more than 4000 dwellings. The 3 buildings G, H and I, 10 to 15 floors high, gather 530 dwellings and needed a renovation, after the question of their demolition has been ruled out. By their location and their layout, these buildings give a capacity of transforming into beautiful dwellings with qualities and comfort. The project of transformation starts from the interior of the dwellings, to give new qualities to the dwellings, by inventoring with precision and care the existing qualities, that should be preserved, and what is missing that must be supplemented.

The addition of wintergardens and balconies in extension of the existing give the opportunity, for each apartment, to enjoy more space, more natural light, more mobility of use and more views.

From the inside, the view on the city of Bordeaux is panoramic and unique, due to the height and to the low topography of the city. It is an extraordinary living situation.

While the high-rise buildings for high-class residences are now defined as examples of a responsible housing for the future, the G, H and I buildings offer the opportunity to reach these qualities immediately, in a generous, economic and sustainable way.

location
Bordeaux, France,
Cité du Grand Parc, Bâtiments G, H, I
year
2011- 2016
type
social housing
client
Aquitanis O.P.H. de la communauté Urbaine de Bordeaux (CUB)
(Social housing operator)
status
under construction
size
SHON: 44 210 m² existing
+ 23 500 m² extensions
(floor area: 68 000m² floor area including wintergardens)
cost
27,2 M€ HT (transformation),
1,2 M€ HT (new dwellings)
architects
Anne Lacaton & Jean-Philippe Vassal associated with Fréderic Druot and Christophe Hutin
architects collaborators
Julien Callot, Marion Cadran, Vincent Puyoo, Marion Pautrot
engineers
SECOTRAP Ingénierie (structure, systems), CESMA (metal structure), CARDONNEL Ingénierie (thermic studies)
works coordination
BATSCOP
program
530 transformed dwellings and 8 new dwellings

The general economy of the project is based on the choice of transforming the existing building without doing important interventions on the existing : the structure, the stairs or the floors and of proceeding by additions and extensions. This approach on economy makes possible to concentrate the resources on generous. These extensions widen the space of use and the mobility inside the dwelling and give the opportunity, as in a house, to have a private outdoor space.
The apartments open on to large wintergardens and balconies, and offer pleasant outdoor spaces, large enough to be fully used : 3,80m deep on the South facades for the buildings H and I buildings and the 2 façades of the building G, only composed by the mono-orientated dwellings.
The existing windows are replaced by large glassed sliding doors, which connect every room of the dwelling to the winter garden.
Interior works are also planned in every dwelling as well as the renovation of the bathrooms and a new electrical installation. In every staircase of 45 dwellings The 2 former elevators serving every staircase of 45 dwellings are replaced by a new bigger one and supplemented by a new elevator built to improve the vertical circulation. On groundfloor, new access halls are done, more opened and transparent, and the gardens in front of the buildings are improved.
The global performance of the building envelope is also improved by the addition of wintergardens and by the insulation of the North facade.
Through this project, the social housing, often criticized heritage, set an example of a relevant and economic transformation that produces - from an existing judged lacking in qualities and seen in a negative way - generous , pleasant and performing dwellings, which renew and reformulate the typologies and the conditions of living, of comfort and of pleasure, and improve the image and attractivity of urban housing.

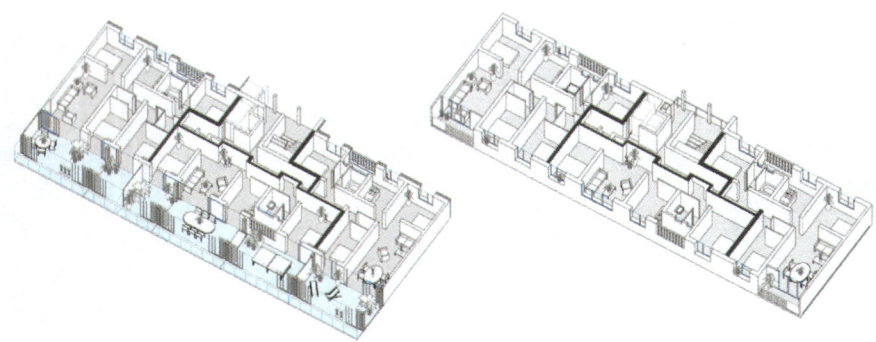

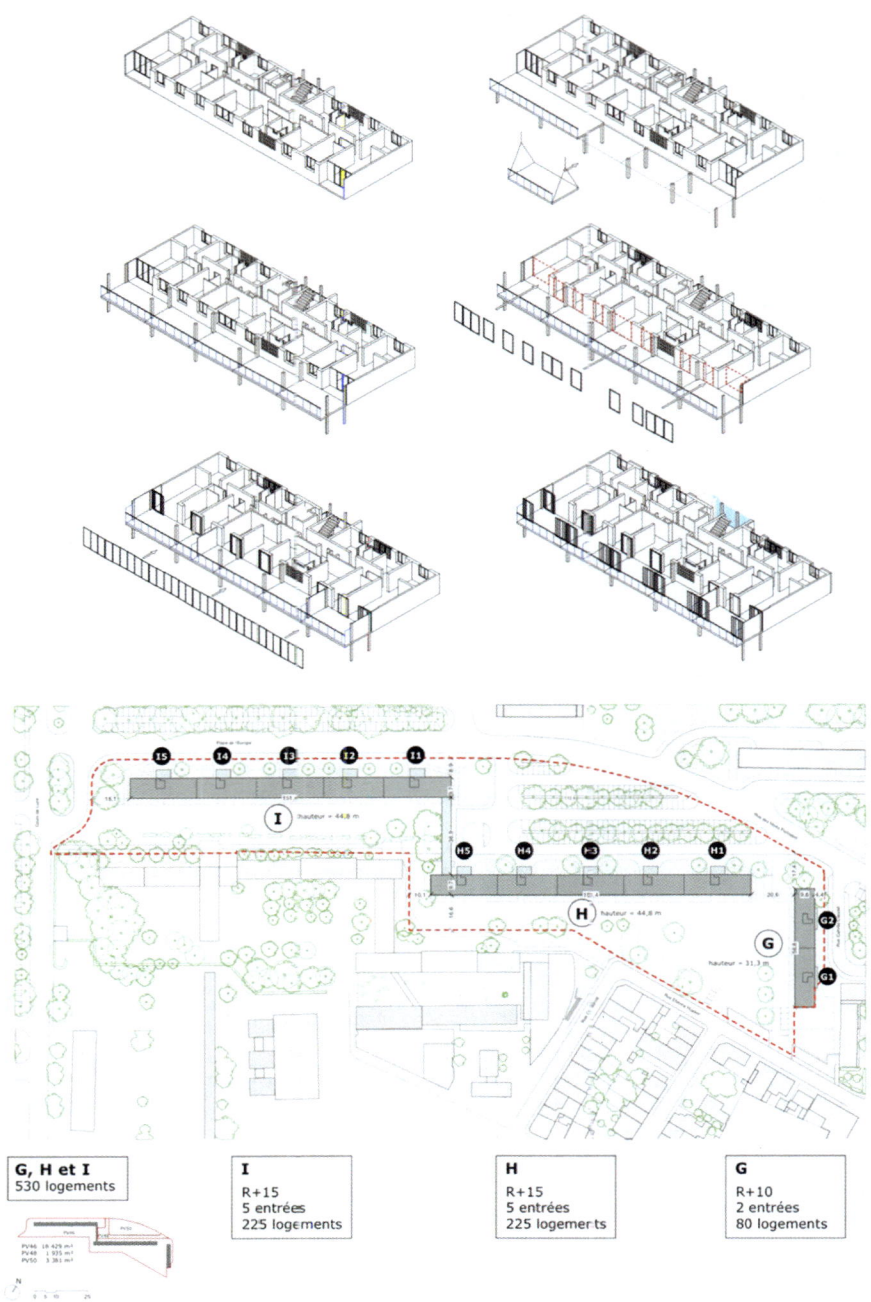

HOUSING TRASFORMATION SAN NAZAIRE

The block of 3 rue des Ajoncs is a part of a highrise estate, La Chesnaie, characteristic of the urban planning of the 70s, based on the massive development of modern housing in the context of providing apartments for all and an optimistic vision of the future.

Today the district has no more attractiveness and is depreciated, towards the inhabitants of the city. The image is degraded.

These situations, here as somewhere else, lead the authorities to demolish, to disintegrate, to drill, to spread, to recompose, to redraw the mass plans, without cares for the existing.

We do not like this method. We think that to demolish is an error, and that we can make differently. Because if we look at the district attentively, objectively, from the inside, we see qualities and capacities there:
- the inhabitants, the green spaces, the beautiful trees,
- the modernity,
- solid constructions, rather well preserved,
- the beautiful views far away in front of,
- an urban situation close to the city center, well connected by transport
- a good management of the buildings by the owner, closer of the inhabitants, in order to solve their problems,
- the conviviality, and often people rooted, attached to their district, but bothered by the bad image which sticks on it.

All this has a value, a sufficient value to consider that the existing situation has assets and precious qualities, which are a consequent support in a radical and positive transformation.

The transformation of the building 3 rue des Ajoncs goes into this attitude, as an action of longer term, which will re - qualify durably housing and all the district.

location
Saint-Nazaire, France
year
competition 2006
completion 2014 & 2016
type
habitat maison/housing
client
Silène
status
built
size
10 282 m²
cost
6,6M€ net
architects
Anne Lacaton & Jean Philippe Vassal with Frédéric Druot
architect collaborator
Julien Callot
construction supervision
Mabire & Reich
Engineering
CESMA (metal structure), PLBI (concrete structure), AREA (systems), Cardonnel (thermic), Guy Jourdan (acoustic), Vincent Pourtau (cost)
Program
R+10 building, 40 transformed dwellings + 40 new dwellings

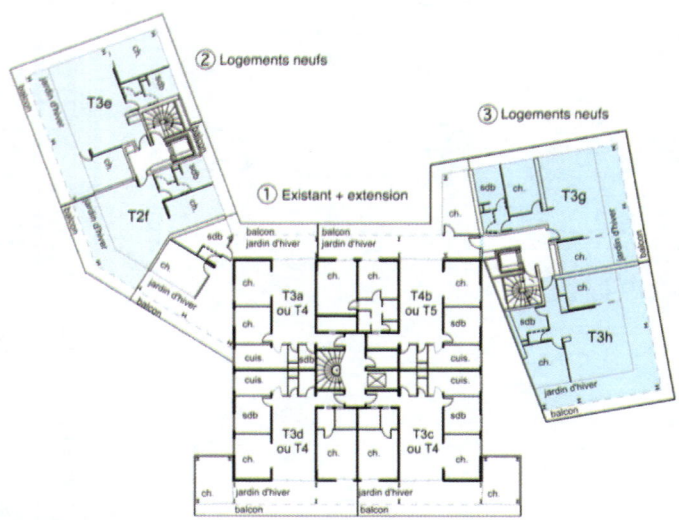

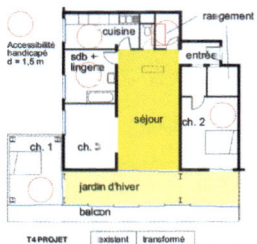

① - Déplacement de la salle de bain dans la chambre 1 (surface 9,4 m2). La salle de bain existante devient rangement
② - Chambre 1 à recréer dans l'extension aux dimensions handicapés (surface 12,9 m2)
③ - Création d'un jardin d'hiver contigu (surface 20,8 m2, largeur 2 m)
④ - Balcon (surface 13,6 m2, largeur 1 m)

- Espace de séjour agrandi
- Salle de bain agrandie et éclairée naturellement
- Surface de rangement doublée
- Plus de lumière naturelle
- Profiter des vues
- Espaces intermédiaires de plain pied
- Double peau habitable et énergétique
- Confort thermique hiver / été
- Réduction coût énergie / charges diminuées
- Accessibilité handicapés de tous les logements

Reuse and transformation in Lacaton & Vassal's architecture

SOCIAL HOUSING MULHOUSE

This project for 14 single-family houses is part of an operation for 61 dwellings created by five teams of architects* in the extended space of a housing estate in Mulhouse.
Our aim is to produce quality houses that are, for the same price, considerably larger than the standardized housing usually met with.
To begin with, the creating of a structure and a cheap and effective simple enveloppe enables us to define, on the loft principle, a maximum surface area and volume with contrasting, complementary and surprising spatial qualities. On the ground floor a post/beam structure in concrete supports a platform at a height of 3 m, upon which horticultural greenhouses are fixed. The frame is in galvanized steel, the walls in transparent polycarbonate. Part of the greenhouse is isolated and heated. The other part constitutes a winter gardne, largely ventilated via the roof and facade. A horizontal sunshade unfurls inside the greenhouse. The greenhouse principle, with its automated climate-control devices, has enabled solutions to the bioclimate to be developped.
Later on, we divide the volume into 14 dwellings**, set crosswise in duplex form, which profit from all the different qualities offered by the diversity of the spaces.

location
Mulhouse, France
year
2005
type
collective housing
client
SOMCO, Mulhouse
status
built
size
2 262 m² (including garages and winter gardens)
average surface area by type :
T5 (175 m2), T4 (175 m2),
T3 (128 m2), T2 (102 m2)
client
SOMCO, Mulhouse
cost
1,05 M€ HT/net (75 000 € HT/net per house) (val. 2004)
architects
Anne Lacaton
& Jean-Philippe Vassal
architects collaborators
David Duchein, David Pradel
engineers
Loeb Ingénierie SA, Cesma, Inotec, Cardonnel, E21

--

* Jean Nouvel, Poitevin & Raynaud, Lewis+Block, Lacaton & Vassal, Shigeru Ban & De Gastines
** 14 council houses for rent / 2 T5, 6 T4, 4 T3, 2 T2

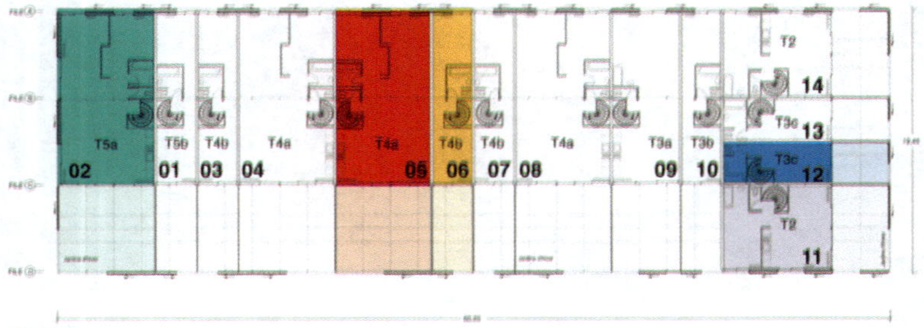

T5a
T5b
T4b
T4a
T4a
T4b
T4b
T4a
T3a
T3b
T2
T3c
T3c
T2
02
01
03
04
05
06
07
08
09
10
14
13
12
11

PLAN R+1

T5a
02
14
T2
T3c
13
T5b
T4b
T4a
T4a
T4b
T4b
T4a
T3a
T3b
11
T2
T3c
01
03
04
05
06
07
08
09
10
12

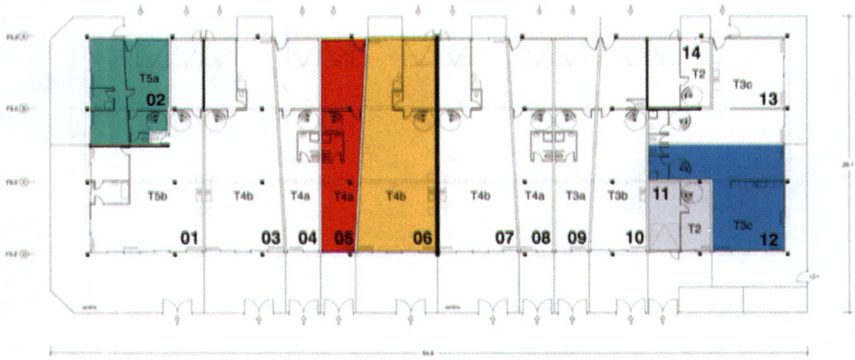

PLAN RDC

ETE / JOUR

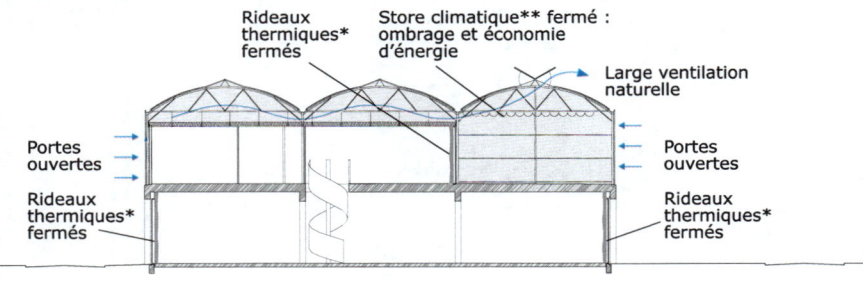

Rideaux
thermiques*
fermés
Store climatique** fermé :
ombrage et économie
d'énergie
Large ventilation
naturelle
Portes
ouvertes
Portes
ouvertes
Rideaux
thermiques*
fermés
Rideaux
thermiques*
fermés

PLAN MASSE

0 5 10 50

HIVER / NUIT

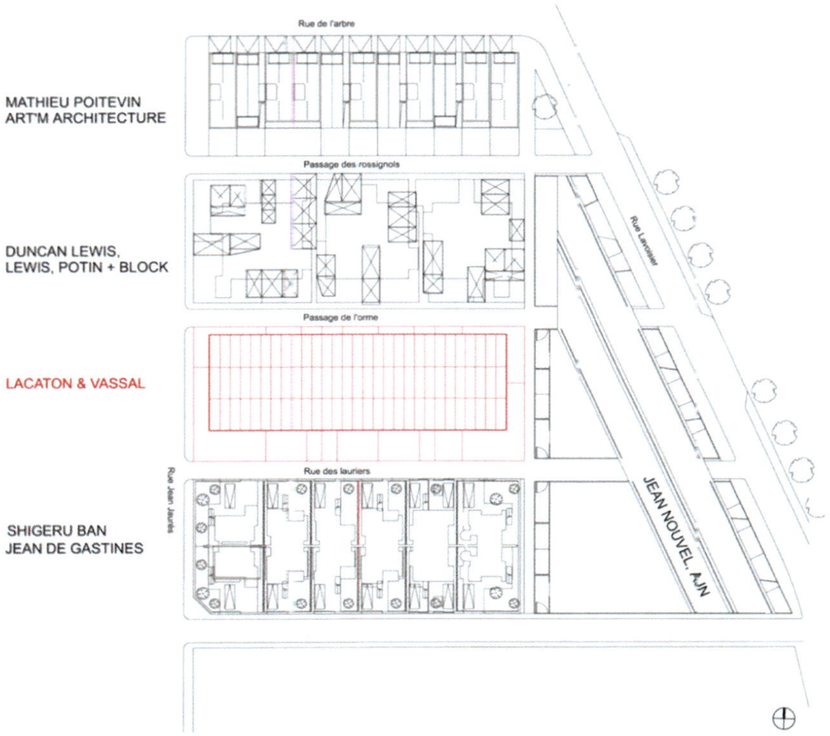

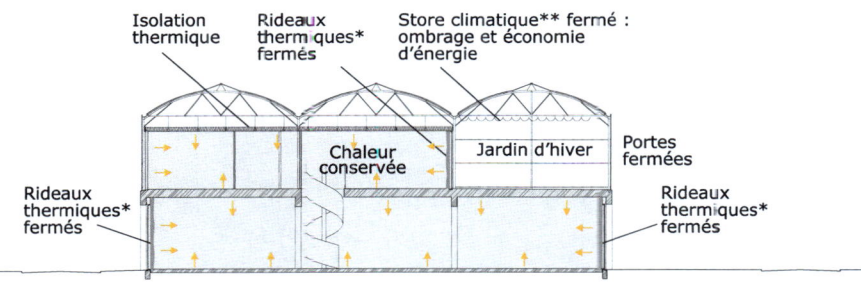

MAISONS AVEC JARDIN D'HIVER A MULHOUSE

* Rideaux thermiques et occultants composés : face extérieure aluminisée réfléchissante + isolant mince en laine mouton + face intérieure tissu

** Ecran mobile (pliable ou enroulable) en tissu léger rayé de bandelettes aluminium réfléchissantes : fait de l'ombre le jour et retient la chaleur la nuit

Reuse and transformation in Lacaton & Vassal's architecture

96 DWELLINGS
CHALON SUR SAÔNE

The project is situated in a modernist neighbourhood of 3 000 dwellings built in the 60's, in Chalon-sur-Saone near the River Saone. It occupies a never built plot at the South edge of the neighbourhood.

The new housing is the opportunity to expand the Park to the South of the site, connecting thus the new development to the northern part of the site. It is that way reinforced as a strong structural element of the Prés-St-Jean district.

The project of 96 dwellings (86 rental dwellings and 10 for accession to ownership) is composed of four buildings independant but following a continuous line implemented along the existing paths of the plot. Their form of "crank" is inspired of the typical original buildings of the masterplan of the 60's.

The buildings are raised above the ground to take account of the flood risk.

The first level of construction is built at 4,50 m above the natural ground (instead of the 1,30 m minimum requested by the law) in order to create transparency, lightness as well as a pleasant space under the construction where gardens or playgrounds can take place. The dwellings, all dual-aspect, are stacked on 2 or 5 storeys above 4,50 m with sometimes duplex apartments in the upper levels.

The construction's footprint is minimum and limited to a few columns and the platforms for the stairs and elevators.

location
Chalon-sur-Saône,
Prés-Saint-Jean, France
year
2015 (2010)
type
social housing
client
OPAC Saône-et-Loire
(Office Public de HLM,
Social housing operator)
status
built
size
14.725 m^2 (including 2.617 m^2 of winter gardens)
cost
11,361 M€ HT/net
architects
Anne Lacaton & Jean-Philippe Vassal
architects collaborators
Emmanuelle Delage, Maud Chevet, Gaëtan Redelsperger, Julien Sage-Thomas
landscape architect
Cyrille Marlin
engineers
TECO (concerte structure and metal structure), CHALEAS ingénierie (technical systems), CARDONNEL (themic studies), Guy Jourdan (acoustics), BERTHET-LIOGIER (roads and utilities), VPEAS (cost estimate)
program
96 new dwellings (86 for rental + 10 for accession to ownership)

The detachment above the ground is comfortable and gives better conditions of calm and better views, towards the lake on one side and towards the city center on the other.
It creates a transparency that gives a great visibility through the plot. Vegetation can continue to grow under the buildings. The field is left in green space, which could be appropriated by the inhabitants, for gardens or playgrounds. Public access is maintained and walking paths are passing through the field.
The car-parking lot is located only on the ground floor and first floor of the first building. From there, the entrances of the three other buildings are reached by walking through the paths and gardens.
The dwelling's space is generous, much bigger than the standards of social housing without any extracost for the construction per dwelling. All the dwellings are dual aspect and all of them have wintergardens and balconies, expanding the living space. This extra space extend the uses and give the possibility to each inhabitant to have a relation to the nature, in front of his home, different of the green spaces on the ground.
Housing should answer to the changes in the lifestyle and people's expectations. Minimum standard for housing is totally unsufficient to give good conditions of living in the city.
In return of new behaviors and the involvement expected from inhabitants in regard to sustainability : most generous housing, exceptional situations however affordable are given.

---------- Limite de propriété

Quartier des Prés Saint-Jean

N

0   50   100   200

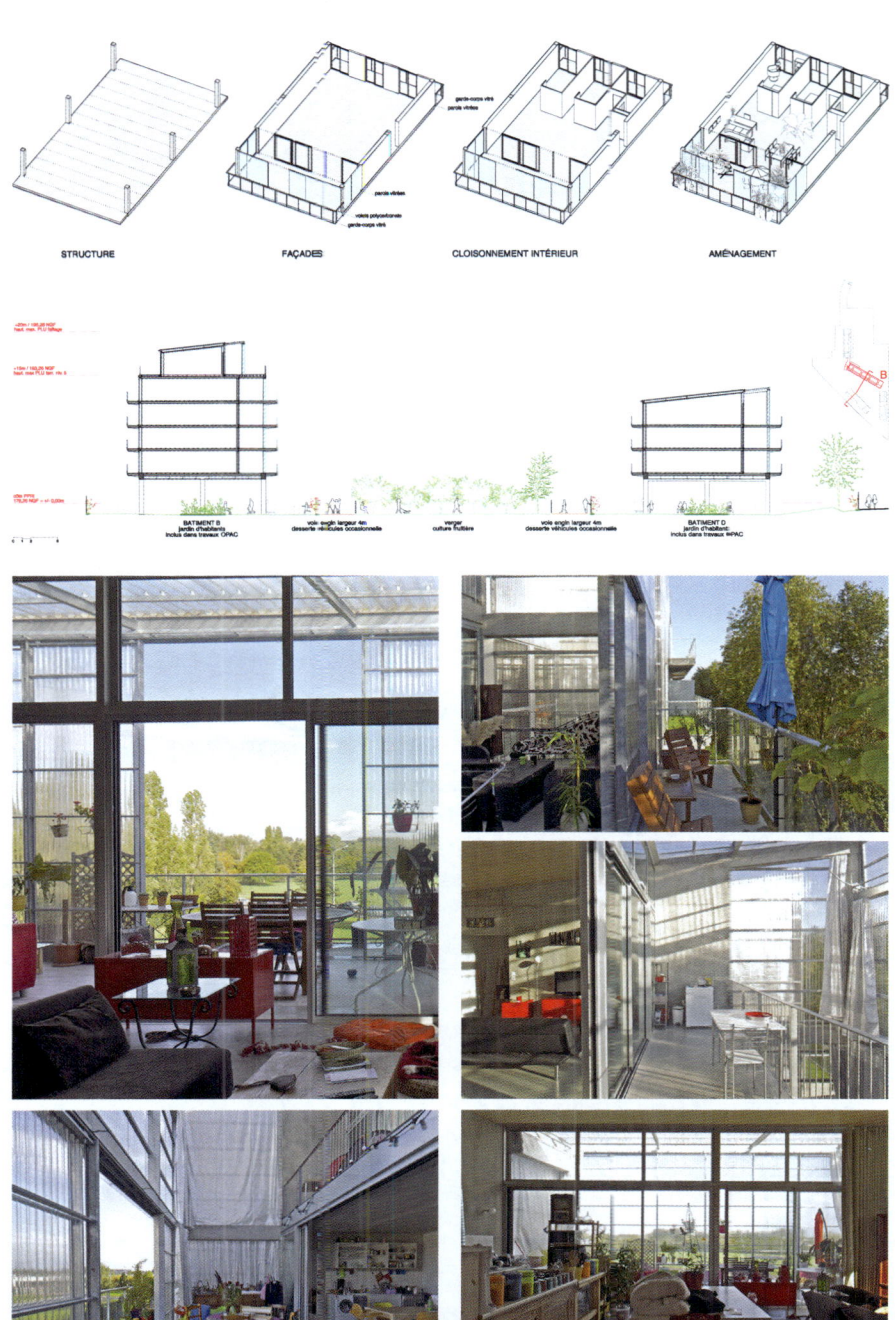

Reuse and transformation in Lacaton & Vassal's architecture

59 DWELLINGS, NEPPERT GARDENS MULHOUSE

A few years after the experience of the Cité Manifeste, the same client SOMCO, commissioned us a new project of social housing in the city of Mulhouse.

Our commun goal was to pursue at least the same aims as the Cité Manifeste : generous dwellings, much bigger than basic standards, however with the same cost per dwelling, in order to rent it as social housing without increasing the rent.

The project is located between Bulher street and Neppert street in Mulhouse, It includes 59 social rental dwellings

The aims of the projetc are first defined in terms of quality of living :
- to create dwellings with surfaces bigger than the standards
- to offer additionnal and intermediate spaces, with different characteristics than traditional rooms in an individual house, that widen the uses, the diversity of spaces and the climatic atmospheres.
- to bring the collective housing close to the qualities of an individual house, in developing outdoor spaces that extend the indoor rooms.
- to optimize the number of dwellings in comparison with the plot capacity, in order to develop an efficient project's economy that allows to build the largest possible surfaces for housing.

location
Mulhouse, France
year
2014 & 2015 (2009)
type
public social housing
status
built
size
size : 8.820 m^2 SHON dwellings (including 2.410 sqm winter gardens) and 93 m^2 shops
client
SOMCO, operator in Social Housing
cost
5,75 M€ net
architects
Anne Lacaton & Jean Philippe Vassal
architects collaborators
Emmanuelle Delage, architecte, chef de projet, Sylvain Godard, architect assistant
architect for implementation
Benjamin Dubreu
engineers
AIA ingénierie (structure béton / concrete structure), E.T.F ingénierie (systems), CARDONNEL ingénierie (thermal calculations), Gui JOURDAN (acoustics)
program
59 logements / 59 dwellings

All the flats, from T1 to T5, are dual-aspect. They offer various plans and typologies of one-story apartments and duplex apartements. The living rooms, south-east oriented, open on to an unoverlooked terrace, that can be fully closed in winter.

hese wintergardens, widely opened in summer, define a bioclimatic system, with a wide natural ventilation, allowing to avoid overheating problems, and create a buffer space in winter, taking advantage of the sun radiation. Besides they offer an extra space for uses in addition to the living rooms

The construction is performing in terms of energy saving.
The constructive system is mostly composed by industrialized elements. The project's concept satisfies the requirements regarding the respect for the environment, the energy saving, and fits to the sustainable development philosophy, including the inhabitants quality of living as a main criteria.

Reuse and transformation in Lacaton & Vassal's architecture   73

STUDENTS AND SOCIAL HOUSING OUCURQ-JAURÈS

The building is located in the 19th district of Paris, in between the Ourcq Canal and the 'Petite ceinture' railroads, today out of use. The district is in full restructuring and many new dwellings are beeing built.
The project includes 98 students dwellings and 30 social dwellings as well as a specialised care home for handicapped adults and 3 shops. It is built along and at the corner of two streets and thus creates a large garden inside the plot. It provides spacious dwellings and gives, as much as possible, the opportunity to the inhabitants to enjoy the two situations: on the garden and on the street. All the 30 social dwellings are dual-aspect or double-oriented. The living rooms and kitchens are on the garden side and open on to a 2,10m deep wintergarden, South or South-East orientated, of 9 to 28 sqm, extended by a 1m deep balcony. The bedrooms and main bathrooms, well glazed, are on the North façade, and open on to a continuous balcony.
The students dwellings, of 19 to 23 sqm have large and high glazed sliding doors. On the street side, they open onto a balcony. On the garden side most of them have a 3,7 sqm wintergarden, extended by a balcony. Inside, the prefabricated bathrooms are optimized to offer more space to the living room.
On the garden side, the ground floor is used by the specialised care home, hosting 6 handicapped residents. The rooms and living spaces benefit the south-east orientation, as well as

location
Paris, France
year
2014
type
housing
status
built
client
Société Immobilière d'Economie Mixte de la ville de Paris
size
6.735 m² SHON/GFA
cost
10,7 M€ HT/ net (2010)
architects
Anne Lacaton & Jean-Philippe Vassal
project manager
Gaëtan Redelsperger
engineers
AIA Paris (structure),
INEX (technical systems, thermic studies),
VPEAS (cost consultant),
Vulcanéo (fire security consultant),
Gui Jourdan (acousticien, acoustics),
Batscop (construction coordinating)
program
3 shops and activities / 30 social dwellings + 98 students dwellins + 1 specialised care home + 3 retails

the use of the garden, a lawn, planted with trees and flowering bushes. The shops occupy the street side all along the façade, only interrupted by the entrances of the residences.

The wintergardens and balconies give to each dwelling a privative outdoor space which offers the possibility to live outside, to have a little garden, such as for a house.

Combined with thermal and shading curtains, the wintergardens are also efficient for the thermal comfort, in winter and in summer, by creating a buffer space with an intermediate climate. This bioclimatic approach, efficient in saving energy, provides at the same time an extra space for extra uses.

Essential to the quality of life in an urban context, these private outdoor spaces bring closer the apartment to the living conditions and pleasure of an individual house.

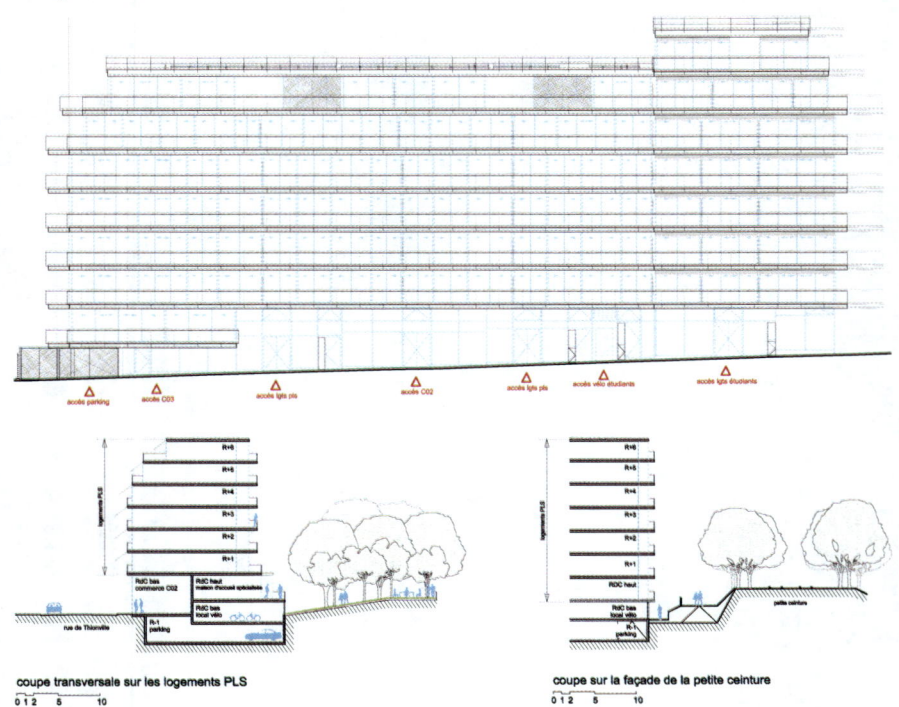

coupe transversale sur les logements PLS

coupe sur la façade de la petite ceinture

Reuse and transformation in Lacaton & Vassal's architecture 79

Reuse and transformation in Lacaton & Vassal's architecture

MANAGEMENT SCIENCES UNIVERSITY BORDEAUX

Implanted in a developing urban context, the University forms a dense, extremely urban nucleus built systematically on the alignment of streets. Four blocks unfold at different levels around a square and a number of arcades and interior courtyards. Each block harbors a department from the second floor up, while the shared services and restaurant occupy the ground and first floor. The structure is carried out with prefabricated elements of bulk concrete-posts, beams and decks of enormous span-thus constituting a supple and economical building system. The totally glazed facades provide abundant natural light, which can be modulated by means of the external blinds, and offer ample views over the city. They also play their part in providing comfort in terms of warmth. In winter the spaces benefit from the input of heat radiation. In summer the blinds provide good protection from the buildup of heat on the facades. The wrap-around outside balconies enable one to go out and take the air to clean the window panes. Six hundred feet of rose bushes are planted there. Decorative and poetic, they provide a delicate touch for the users and local inhabitants of the district and recall the charm of the little gardens of the surroundings. Another form of comfort, signifying the quality of the space, the light and the seasons.

location
Bordeaux, France,
year
2008
type
education
client
Mairie de Bordeaux
status
built
size
19.570 m^2
cost
21 M€ HT/net
architects
Anne Lacaton & Jean-Philippe Vassal
architects collaborators
Emmanuelle Delage,
Benjamin Dubreu, Frédéric Hérard, David Pradel
landscape architect
Cyrille Marlin
engineers
Setec, Secotrap, engineers, Lionel Dubernard, cost estimate, Vulcanéo, fire security consultant
Roses: Meilland

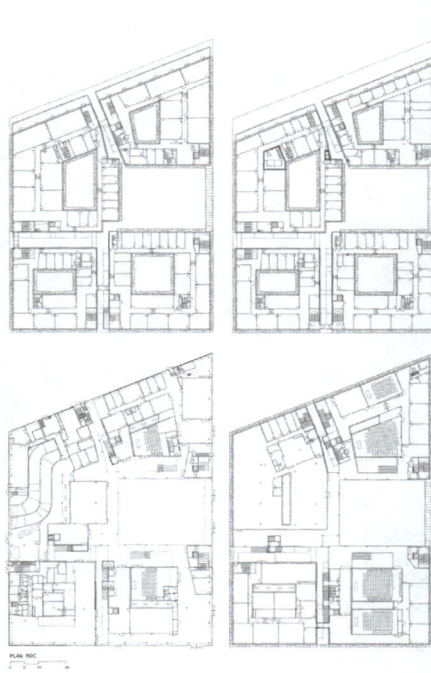

84   Re-Invent

Reuse and transformation in Lacaton & Vassal's architecture

SCHOOL OF ARCHITECTURE NANTES

In building a structure of great capacity, the project design comes up with a scheme capable of creating a set of rich and diverse situations of interest to the School of architecture, the city and the landscape. Three decks at nine, sixteen and twenty-two meters above the natural ground level, served by a gentle sloping external ramp, progressively put the ground surface of the city in touch with the sky overhead. A lightweight steel structure redivides the height of these main levels. It enables the spaces devoted to the program to be generously installed and creates a system adapted to their extension and their future evolution. Linked to the spaces of the program are ample, double-height volumes with non-attributed functions, the transparent facades of which harness the sun's rays and vouchsafe the indoor climate. On the initiative of the students, teachers or visitors, these spaces become the locus of possible appropriations, events and programming. At any one moment the adaptation of the school to new interventions and its reconversion are possible. Like a pedagogical tool, the project questions the program and the pratices of the school as much as the norms, technologies and its own process of elaboration.

location
Nantes, France
year
2009
type
education
client
Ministère de la culture et de la communication - DRAC Pays de Loire
status
built
size
15.150 m^2 basic program + 4.430 m^2 extra space + 5.305 m^2 accessible outside terraces
cost
17,75 M€ HT/net (val. 2008)
architects
Anne Lacaton & Jean-Philippe Vassal
architects collaborators
Florian De Pous, Frédéric Hérard, and Julien Callot, Lisa Schmidt-Colinet, Isidora Meier
engineers
Setec Bâtiment (concrete structure, systems), CESMA (metal structure), E2I (cost estimate), Jourdan (acoustics), Vulcanéo (fire security)
program
school of architecture for 1.000 students

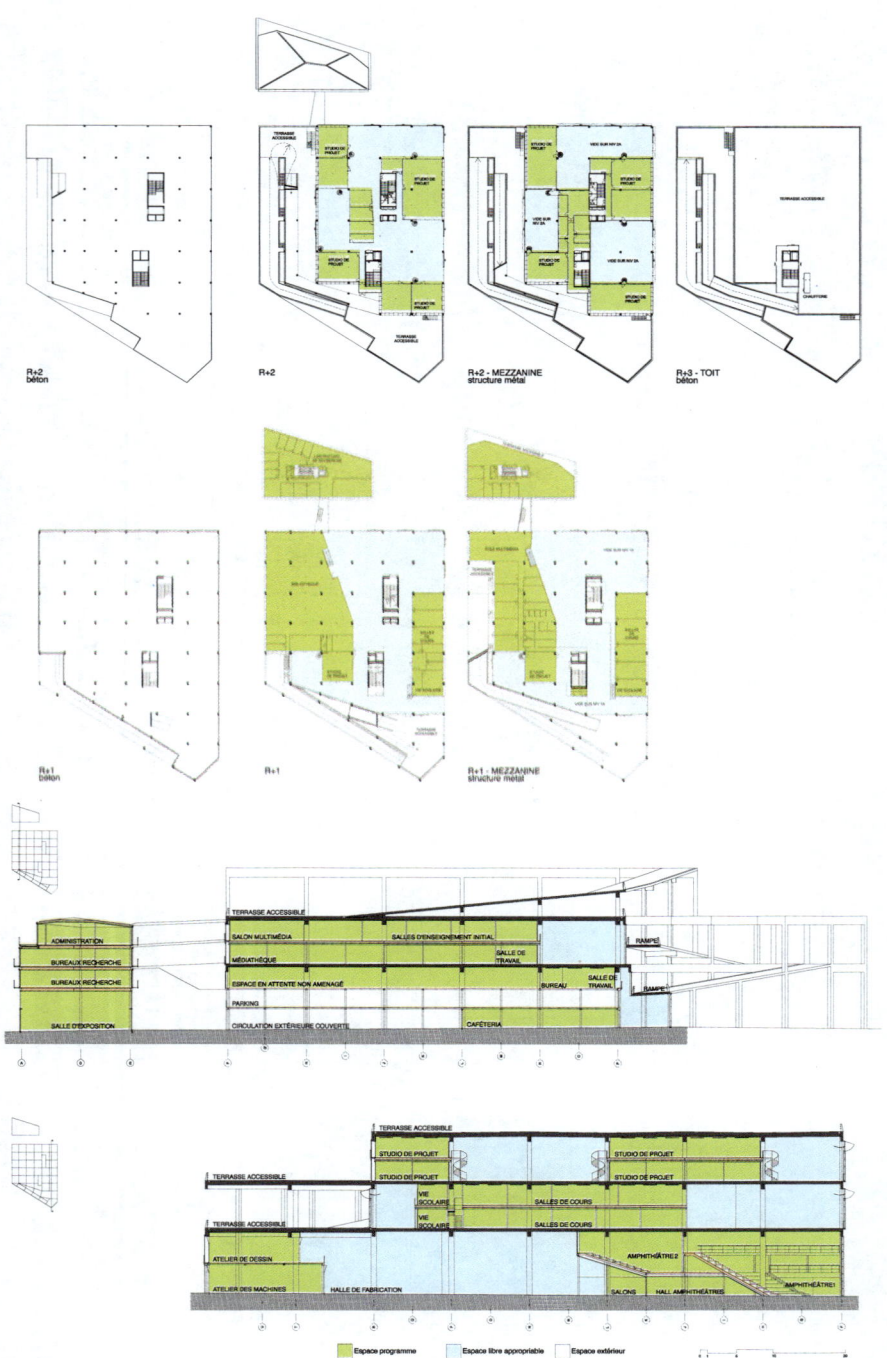

POLYVALENT THEATER
LILLE

The multi-purpose hall " Le Grand Sud " is part of the 28 ha restructuring of the Arras Europe sector in Lille. A place of cultural diffusion on the city scale, it also hosts the new district's non-profit organizations and events.

The project "slips" under a vast accessible roof formed by a sloping public garden, created by the development of the district.

In the volume of variable height, following the slope of the garden, the auditorium takes up the central area. Freed from load-bearing elements, it is equipped with movable and modular bleachers and a staging area in the forefront.

Surrounding this is a large, 2500m² space at park level, for the rest of the public functions.

The space is flexible and versatile, thanks to a system of big curtains and acoustic folding doors, easily manipulated, on a system of rails, allowing numerous capacities and configurations.

The volume " disappears " under the garden, and reveals only two facades:
- In the lower part, big sliding windows, 2,50 m high, that are fully openable
- In the upper part, the ETFE facades are composed of 2 m thick greenhouses, containing flower planters and equipped with an automatic system of natural ventilation, watering, shading curtains, etc. to enable climate control.

Perpendicular to the central room, a mobile facade can open along its entirety, realizing the room's maximal extension towards the park, creating a scenic backdrop.

location
Lille, France
year
competition 2009
completion 2013
type
education
client
Ville de Lille
status
built
size
3.791 m² SHON
cost
6,932 M€ net
(+1,256 M€ scenography)
architects
Anne Lacaton & Jean-Philippe Vassal
chief project
Emmanuelle Delage
construction supervision
Vincent Ducatez
engineers
Batiserf (concrete), Cesma (metal structure), Inex (mechanical systems), Michel Forgue (cost), Vulcanéo (fire security consultant), Gui Jourdan (acoustics), Architecture & techniques (scenography)
program
polyvalent theater

Plan RDC

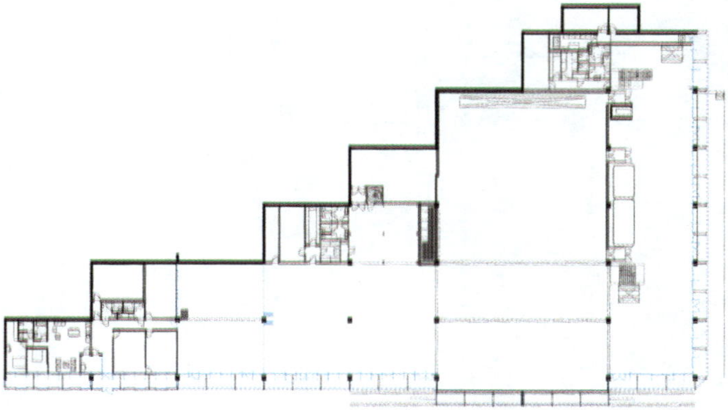

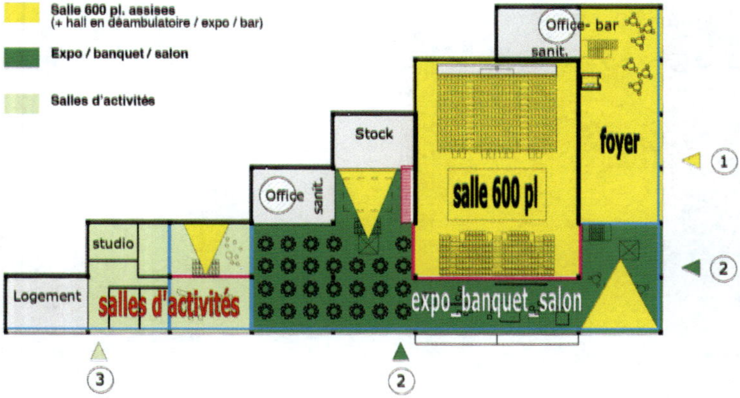

Salle 600 pl. assises
(+ hall en déambulatoire / expo / bar)
Expo / banquet / salon
Salles d'activités
Office- bar
sanit.
Stock
foyer
salle 600 pl
Office
sanit.
studio
Logement
salles d'activités
expo_banquet_salon
1
2
3
2

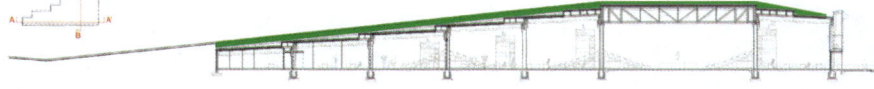

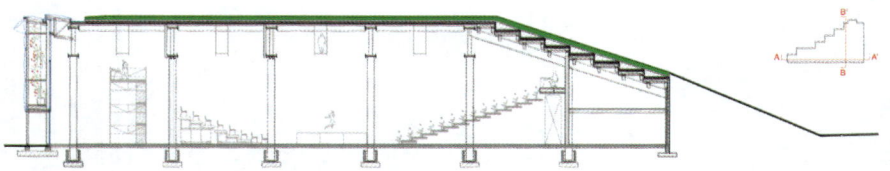

Coupe longitudinale AA'

Coupe transversale BB'

FRAC NORD-PAS DE CALAIS

The FRAC houses regionally assembled public collections of contemporary art.
These collections are conserved, archived and presented to the public through on site exhibitions and by loans to both galleries and museums.
The North region FRAC is located on the site of Dunkerque port in an old boat warehouse called Halle AP2.
The halle AP2 is a singular and symbolic object. Its internal volume is immense, bright, impressive. Its potential for uses is exceptional.
To implant the FRAC, as a catalyst for the new area, and also to keep the halle in its entirety becomes the basic idea of our project.
To achieve this concept, the project creates a double of the halle, of the same dimension, attached to the existing building, on the side which faces the sea, and which contains the program of the FRAC.
The new building juxtaposes delicately without competing nor fading. The duplication is the attentive response to the identity of the halle; Under a light and bioclimatic envelope, a prefabricated and efficient structure determines free, flexible and evolutionary platforms, with few constraints, fit to the needs of the program.
The transparency of the skin allows to see the background vision of the opaque volume of the artworks reserves.

location
Dunkerque, France
year
competition 2009
completion 2013 - 2015
type
social housing
client
Communauté Urbaine de Dunkerque
status
built
size
11.129 m^2 net :
- 9.157 m^2 new building
- 1.972 m^2 existing halle
cost
12 M€ net
architects
Anne Lacaton & Jean-Philippe Vassal
architects collaborator
Florian De Pous
project manager
Camille Gravellier
construction supervision
Yuko Ohashi
engineers
Secotrap (structure, mechanical systems), Cesma (metal structure), Vincent Pourtau (cost), Vulcanéo (fire security consultant), Gui Jourdan (acoustics), Cardonnel (thermal studies)
program
artwork reserves, exhibition rooms, education

The public footbridge (previously planned along the facade) which crosses the building becomes a covered street entering the halle and the internal facade of the FRAC.
The halle AP2 will remain a completely available space, which can work either with the FRAC, in extension of its activities, (exceptional temporary exhibitions, creation of large scale works, particular handlings) or independently to welcome public events (concert, fairs, shows, circus, sport) and which enriches the possibilities of the area. The functioning of each of the buildings is separated, or combined.
The architecture of the halle and its current quality make sufficient minimal, targeted and limited interventions. Thanks to the optimization of the project, the budget allows the realisation of the FRAC and the setting up of conditions and equipment for public use of the halle AP2.
The project so creates an ambitious public resource, of flexible capacity, which allows work at several scales from everyday exhibitions to large-scale artistic events, of regional but also european and international resonance, which consolidates the redevelopment of the port of Dunkerque.

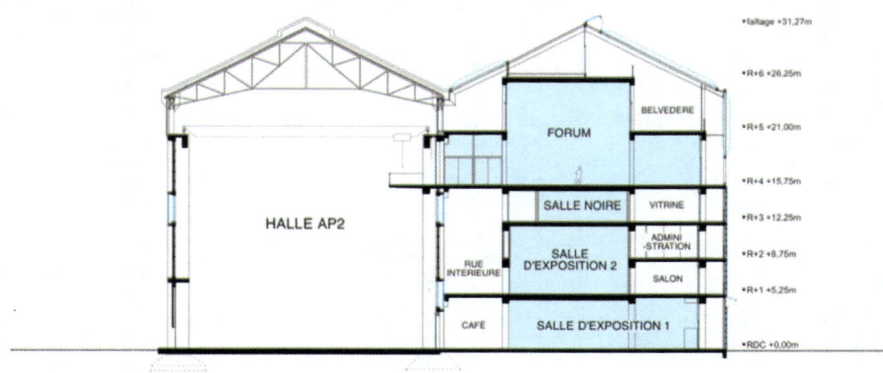

PARCOURS VERTICAL DE VISITE

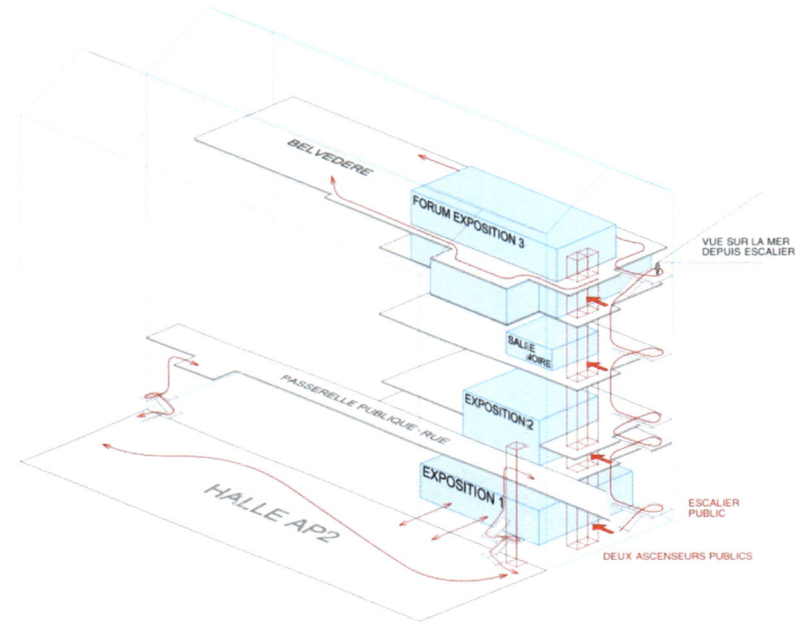

Reuse and transformation in Lacaton & Vassal's architecture   103

Reuse and transformation in Lacaton & Vassal's architecture

PALAIS DE TOKYO
SITE FOR CONTEMPORARY CREATION

The thing that has made the Palais de Tokyo so special and contributed so much to its reputation since reopening in 2001, in addition of course to its artistic programs, is the broad freedom it offers to the visitors and to the works of art they flock to see. This freedom creates a general feeling of a place designed for sharing and debating ideas, with a free and transparent ambiance of well being, and a place its visitors can make their own.

Ten years after reopening to the public, the new phase of development with the extension of the area occupied to the entire space of its four levels is remaining faithful to its role as a site created to promote access to an awarness of contemporary art.

This internal expansion enable the institution to fully utilize the impressive height, depth and adaptability of its vast spaces.

The "contemporary arts district" is a place with "many and varied offerings", a lively place of leisure, "where the works on display challenge but can be challenged in return, rather than canonized", a place of "diversity" and much more. Very open and welcoming to the public and to the local neighborhood, it host exhibitions, events, films, music, fashion, a bookstore, a café-restaurant and shops. The public dimension is the primary focus of this facility dedicated to contemporary art. The exceptionally long opening times, the variety of things to do and see here, a familiar and more relaxed atmosphere have all contrib-

location
Paris, France
year
completion 2012 - 2014
type
culture
client
Ministère de la Culture et de la Communication, délégation aux arts plastiques / OPPIC
status
built
size
16.500 m^2
cost
13 M€ net
architects
Anne Lacaton & Jean-Philippe Vassal
architects collaborator
Maud Chevet, Dimitri Messu, Bartolo Santos, Chloé De Smet, Joanne Rasse, Ambroise Bonal
project manager
Camille Gravellier
construction supervision
Yuko Ohashi
engineers
AIA ingénieries, Adrien Paporello, CESMA, Mr. Stanik (steel structure), INEX, Stéphane Coumailleau (electrical studies), INEX, Clément Triadou (mechanical studies)
program
site for contemporary creation (exhibition rooms, workshops and storage)

uted to developing a loyal and eager public. People like to slow down and take their time in this place.

The spirit of the project and the broad range of activities planned for the Palais de Tokyo require the maximum possible available space while enabling each activity a broad measure of independence in the way it can use this space.

The full use of the entire space facilitate and enhance an increased and diverse number of activities and events, with no down time, never closing.

The approach taken to space in this project enable very flexible management of the different areas of the facility and its rich programs, all offered in a skillfully organized series of rooms, spaces, and time frames for various uses; all within a container as vast as possible. Though open, it can easily be temporarily partitioned and reconfigured into an immense space or divided into smaller spaces.

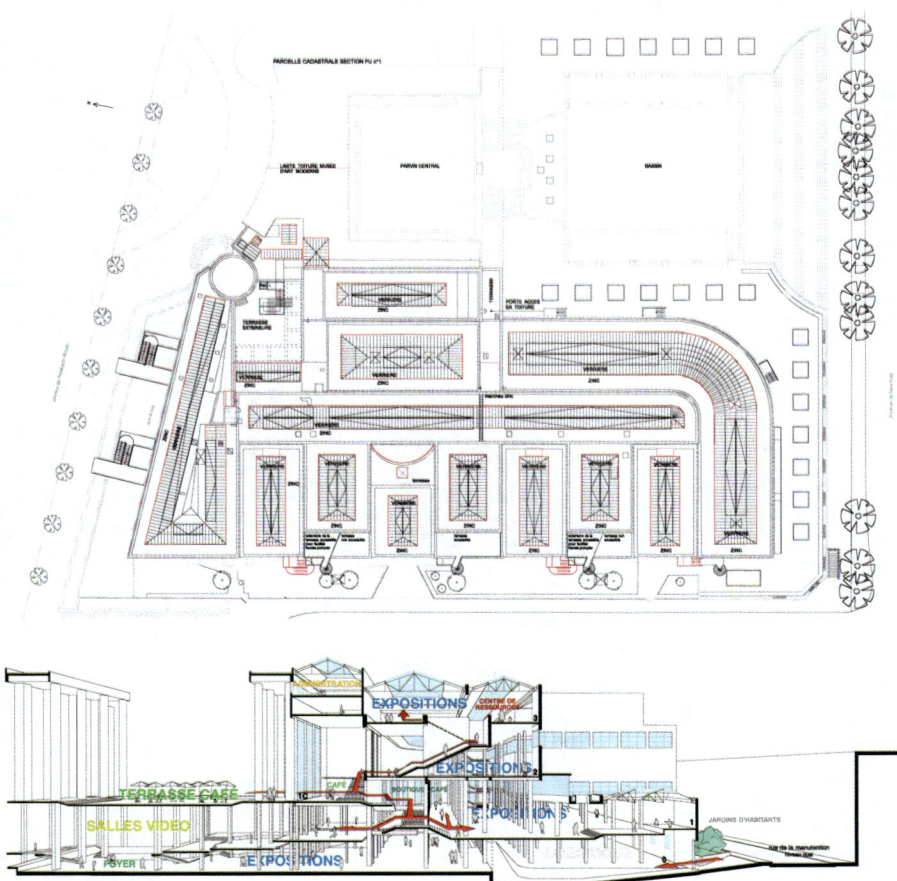

Reuse and transformation in Lacaton & Vassal's architecture

Reuse and transformation in Lacaton & Vassal's architecture 113

Seeking reality
Interview with Lacaton & Vassal

The interview is the partial development of some conversations that took place during numerous meetings and whilst collaborating with Lacaton & Vassal on various research courses we shared in the ecourbanlab in Alghero at the Department of Architecture, Design and Urban Planning. In between lessons and conferences organised by the lab, but also at the inauguration of exhibitions of their works, or during visits to their studio, discussions often dwelt on some of the basic principles of their way of thinking, teaching and constructing architecture. Re-inventing, transforming, re-using what exists for the pleasure of living were confirmed in Lacaton & Vassal's responses, as necessary principles for building a solid relationship between architecture and user, but also architecture and city. In their words, it is possible to grasp a concept of sustainability that develops in terms of simple relations with the environment. A way of using technologies and materials that recall agricultural and industrial contexts in support of a simple, basic kind of architecture conceived to seek the potential of space experienced in its temporal dimension, and which responds to the requirements of the individual using it. In their replies architecture's capacity to adapt is emphasised, obtained by giving the project a dimension open to possibilities, also for future use as yet uncertain and not definitive. This taking on of responsibility means for Lacaton & Vassal adapting planning to the different contexts, delivering its results into the hands of a future time. In the dialogue that follows architectural research clearly emerges that is non-representative but effectual to the substance and structurality of phenomena. Architecture that constantly regenerates by means of its own critical attitude, posing a continuous challenge to the conditions and cognition itself of reality.

Massimo Faiferri | *The word "re-invent" offers a common key to many of your projects, could you elaborate on that?*
Jean Philippe Vassal | Yes, exactly, in this case the right word would be not invent, but "re-invent". The "re" means that you have to start from something, it means we invent from something.
Anne Lacaton | The prefix "re" is useful, we can use it to create new meanings especially if you link it with other words, for example, re-invent inhabitation.

JPV Also re-inventing architecture.
AL | Doing something new with what we already have.

MF *The Palais de Tokyo is a good example of how to re-invent in architecture.*
JPV Yes, at the same time, re-inventing is also "doing with". Like in the house at Cap Ferret or the transformation of the Bordeaux housing project. If you think about Place Léon Aucoc, the one where we didn't do anything, that is also a way of reinventing. Doing nothing can be an act of architecture. For that square doing nothing was the project, we assumed it as a project and we were paid for it. It is another way of considering what architecture is.

MF | You have been dealing with different housing projects, in different places and situations. What are the differences between them?

JPV I think the purpose was always the same. We believe in modern space, having in mind some references to Modernism in architecture. I am thinking about Mies and Aalto's housing projects and the quality of the space proposed by International Style. You can achieve this aim working in different ways as we did for different projects. For example, the idea of transformation is applied differently in different situations. The objective is to push the situation to its maximum, which was the aim of Modern architecture at some point. You can also design from scratch still with the same principles. In the end, the results are the same, too. In some cases, when you work on the existing, the outcomes are much more impressive than if you start from scratch because the addition can add value to the current situation. "Doing with" means you add to something, and the addition creates more than when there was no addition.

AL | Yes, there is added-value in it. Anyway, the situations are also different. In the project for Chalon-sur-Saône it was very quickly obvious that we could make better use of the ground, because we had a lot of empty ground around the site. Starting with the same goals, observation of the situations creates some differences, some complexities, and some inclinations that give a unique character to any project.

JPV I In a way, this approach is a sort of re-interpretation of Modernism. The tabula rasa approach has already been experienced, and with mistakes - the big slabs, for example. Anyway, even if the approach was wrong, they managed to achieve interesting spaces. This is what we can keep.

Of course, our approach to the existent is completely different. We want to keep it but the new, the additions, should have the quality of modern architecture.

MF | This means that the same idea of transformation can be applied differently in different situations?

JPV I In a way, yes. In fact, the inhabited space of the house in Cap Ferret is the same as for many other projects.

AL | In that case the trees and the location make the difference but the plan of Cap Ferret is not very different from other plans.

JPV I In fact each time it is a case study. You can apply the concept to a place with trees, to the city, a ten-floor building or to the top of a building. It is practically the same space but adapted, confronted and changed by the existing situation.

MF | *So it seems you are linked more with Aalto's Modernism than Le Corbusier's...*
AL | Yes, Aalto is less dogmatic, more connected to places and people. Maybe that makes the difference.
JPV | For me house space is a sort of Modernist reinterpretation of the cave. We no longer have mountains or nature, now the territory is the existing city. We can generate new creative situations with very few materials. That means that with nearly nothing you can do something. You create an inhabited space.

MF | *In what other ways can architecture be in close touch with people?*
JPV | Inhabiting is the connection. To be part of the space. For me the big difference between architecture and sculpture is the fact that somebody is part of the space, somebody is living in it.
AL | We often say that inhabiting is the word common to all projects. Inhabiting is what can characterize all architecture. I am not sure that the English word inhabiting corresponds to "habiter" in French. Habiter is a concept. "Habits" in French means clothes, so "Habiter" is an extension of clothes, something you wrap yourself in to make you comfortable. Sometimes, you have to build it, other times it already exists. Not everyone can see it, so architects help to say OK, if we change this, then you can inhabit the space, you can be somewhere, do something and have the space around you.
JPV | That is a strong concept. I experienced it when I was in the desert; there was still a strong relationship with space although space there is infinite. There is one line, the sand, and sky and this can be a house.
AL | Even in such situations people tend to create domestic space around them, without anything.
JPV | I think what we call a loft is also interesting. The loft is an existing space, and you just use it. With a loft, you put your things in and you use the space. And you find your intimacy. It is really a question of space. In Africa, the desert is a loft.
AL | At this moment space is what we are creating sitting at the table, not the wall or the rooms.
JPV | And the space changes when we move into the other room.

MF | *It seems to me that your work is really a way to create opportunities, not to define a specific way to use them.*
JPV | We should not forget how to build, how to make a roof, a floor, but there are also other materials that are situations. House materials are just not steel, concrete, glass. Cities, the landscape are also materials. In a forest, the trees, the soil and the sun are materials. In Africa, I had a sort of insight. In a context like the desert, where you have nothing, you see these people

looking for shade, building a hat with branches and cloth because it is too warm and sunny. If you think of the same concept transposed to Europe, then it is urbanism at any scale.

AL | It is a question of people and relations - each time you introduce other elements you define another space, and so on. It is interesting to see how space is a collection of an infinite number of situations. The role of architecture is to enable this never-ending set of situations.

JPV | It is still to build something. It is still construction. You build something with the situations, and you can incorporate very traditional ways of creating architecture also, you can mix these two things.

AL | You build something that allows the freedom to use it in different ways.

JPV | For example, if you think about Albert Frey's project in the desert, the house is built in the rock. You have the rock, some corrugated aluminium on the roof and then he places a light switch on the rock.

AL | It is interesting because he was not constrained by space, he could have chosen to build on the side of the rock, but he decided that the rock was one thing and the construction something else and the two elements had to overlap.

JPV | In this work, you have everything: the use of what exists, the "doing with", a sort of sense of humour (the switch on the rock), and an incredible richness. So "building with" does not mean you have to build what was already there, you can add something so that you produce something else.

MF | Where does the quality of architecture lie?

JPV | Our objectives have a lot to do with ambition. For us today spaces are extremely restricted and what we really need is to open up to give more freedom. At the same time, it is also about the disappearance of architecture. When architecture disappears, then you really have more architecture.

AL | For example in the house at Cap Ferret you don't see a lot of architecture, you see a white landscape.

MF | How much does the cost of a building influence its quality?

JPV | We don't need to reduce our ambitions on the grounds of financial constraints. We have to work in a cleverer way within the limits. Being a citizen also means not wasting money. When there are costs for some buildings, of course we have to do the maximum within the cost forecast.

AL | It is very important to respect the right relationship between what you are doing and reasonable costs. Nowadays, there is never a lot of money for buildings, except for the iconic ones; the proper attitude is to not complain but take advantage of the situations, respecting what a client could reasonably spend. The question is what can we do without compromising on intentions. This is what we did for example with Maison Latapie. We had great ambi-

tions for that house; we wanted to be generous, providing wide, high-quality space. The space needed to be much better than a smaller standard house. We were very committed because the budget was low. Since this project, we have really worked hard to understand how it works with the cost of things and what really does it. It is not all about calculation. It is more than that. It is the intelligence of the design. You understand that sometimes doing something has a certain cost, doing the same thing another way costs less, getting the same quality and function. You make a comparison and often see that it costs more when the details are not very clever, or the solutions are too complicated. Moreover, making things complicated is not very interesting.
JPV | You consider the money a challenge, a kind of fight. Sometimes the conditions are so extreme, but then you can really design something different. I daresay that this is almost the definition of beauty. Beauty occurs when there is a moment when you find the right way to get out of a contest between very difficult situations. At the end, the building will be the expression of this fight.

MF | Nowadays there is a lot of emphasis on iconic buildings and on the symbolism issue. I have recently visited the Louis Vuitton Foundation building, and I was wondering whether architecture should really represent something? A brand, an idea, an economic or political power?
JPV | In our first projects the question of symbolism was an issue but, step by step, we have found the concept more and more inappropriate, even if it can sometimes be exciting. We are much more interested in a poetic approach than the demonstration issue. We are not in times of Cathedrals or Palaces; in democracy there should be common sense, people should understand things and not get involved in a sort of mistake that might be the symbolism of some buildings. For example, we have many problems with buildings dealing with memory. We generally like Renzo Piano's work, but we don't appreciate the project in New Caledonia. There are many cases; I'm just taking this Piano project as an example because we really like his work, but not in this case. Perhaps people like it, but we feel it is the transposition of old traditional values that we understand not to be as delicate as it should be.
AL | Our position is against architecture as a means of representation of society or power. According to many sociologists, some philosophers and artists, people need symbolism and monuments. The real question is why should this role be supported by architecture? It is too strong. There is no reason why a building for a theatre, museum or school should become a symbol.
JPV | Memory should be in books and films. That is much more scientific than placing it in a building. We have had some projects, competitions, in which we dealt with this issue; but when you place it at the level of architec-

ture, with one monument, then it does not work. At the Palais of Tokyo we didn't think we needed to add anything, because artists would have come; at the School of Architecture in Nantes, the students and the teachers would have come; in the housing projects, inhabitants would have come. There is no reason to make a demonstration of anything. Very few projects have something else to give. For example, the Café in Vienna, but also the trees around the building for the School of Management in Bordeaux. There were some unbuilt projects where we thought we had to add something. Like the one for the Architecture Foundation in London, where we put a big statue inside the building, not on the top of it - something you could touch. In the project for the museum of Guangzhou in China there were the five huge rams. On some occasions, there could be something more to give, but we try not to make it a symbol. The statue in London and the rams in Guangzhou could not be identified as symbols. You could feel them, touch them, they existed. They acted at different levels, so if you read them as one of the levels of the space, level by level, then you could reconstruct the whole. In both the cases, the statues were just a fragment of the space, not the total space.

AL | In both the cases of London and China, the brief required an icon linked to the history. We dealt with the request, that is why we thought about the statues, but it is not the building itself which is a ram. It is a building and inside there is a figure which could be the icon. So it is not the architecture itself that is an icon, it is something else. We do not see the icon as a literal figure.

JPV | Let's think about the work of Frank Gehry - when we were students we used to look at Frank Gehry's first projects like the houses in Malibou, built with very standard pieces of wood in a very rational and precise way. In the building for the DZ Bank, where there is a statue of the head of a horse associated with the Nazi period (it was not really accepted, then he changed it a little), there was still the complexity of form inside, while outside the building was very simple. After this project, I think his approach totally changed. The building itself was an icon.

MF | *If you think about your recent projects, do you feel that each project develops new ideas or are there any recurring concepts that persist?*

JPV | It is a combination of both. We cannot forget what we have done before. Each time we start a new adventure with new people, new programs, new context but, at the same time, there are persisting elements from our past projects. We could compare design with research on a case study. The case study is always there in the different projects, at the house in Cap Ferret, in a new building or in a transformation project. We could call it generic space that becomes unique because it has been confronted with a special situation.

AL | A case study is not just a house. It is more a model of freedom and generosity - of what architecture can produce with minimum materials.

JPV | If we take the image of the case study, for a block of 15 floors and perhaps 20 meters in length, like in Bordeaux, each unit is important, so we have 500 case studies assembled. There, what we really consider is not the building itself but the unit, the unit has to be at its maximum. Then you have an addition of units, it might be a tower, a slab or just a villa, but the unit is always the reference point. We are never creating a building for 500 families but a building for one family 500 times.

MF| *What are the design principles your projects constantly research?*

JPV | What we like is the sense of accumulation. If you consider the unit, you can consider the city and all the stratifications of spaces. If you consider the unit, then it is like a brick from which you can follow on to the city and the landscape. Coming back to the unit means always coming back to the dimension of the body, of one body, of the human being. We think it makes sense to consider the city this way, instead of seeing it in a global way. It is important because we can go back to each one, with the precision that each one deserves. If you consider the 500 people as a whole, you forget about them.

AL | When we consider different scales, there is no great hierarchy of values for them. The different scales have the same value. Large scale, small scale, there is not one that is more important than another. The last scale is the sum of little scales, a multiplication of the little scales.

MF| *What are the design principles you would like to investigate in the future?*

AL | We would like to emphasize this concept of the addition, that is, creating new places starting from the existing place. We realise it is very difficult to do. There is great potential in developing cities on the grounds of these concepts. Case by case, the principle could be applied to transformation, extension and densification processes. The challenge is to keep the new and old layers together and to add more layers.

MF| *You were talking about your experience in China. Do you think the same principle could be applied there, where the history of the city is completely different from Europe?*

AL | We have only done one competition in China. We were invited, we liked the brief, we found the location interesting and we accepted the invitation. It not something that we are going to develop.

JPV | Anyway, also in that competition, we did not really reflect on whether the local people would have liked the architecture or not. We tried to understand the needs and the situations and we proposed the project. In a way, it is similar in Europe with the issue of participation of the inhabitants. On one hand architects should listen to people, understand the situation. On the other hand, it is up to them to create a new situation through which participation can be possible. It means you have to open up to some possibilities. For Maison Latapie, the discussion was about a single house, which was a normal house. We had a certain amount of money, not a lot, but we considered we were able to build up to 300 square meters. At that point, the discussion could change. The architect has to change the basis of the discussion. If you start the discussion without this first step, you do not share anything.

AL | We don't conceive participation in terms of a collection of needs of the people, as a base to the project. It is important that everyone has his role according to his skills. The inhabitant is not an architect, he should talk about desires, wills and needs. On the other hand, the architect has to take the responsibility to fulfil the expectations of people, bringing in something else that is architecture. It is not about giving the feeling to people that they have done the project themselves. It is much better if everyone emphasises his role in the best way, so if you are an inhabitant you must be the most demanding inhabitant ever and not start to be an architect. Of course, the architect has to take care of what the inhabitant requires, but he has also to give more.

JPV | Sometime the project seems to already be done by the politics or the inhabitants. They just ask the architect to do the technical part or change the form or colour. Most of the time these situations are extremely problematic and if you refuse to find a solution, you just work within the problem. What is interesting is to solve the problem, open up the situation, create greater volume and then listen to everybody's wishes.

AL | In some cases people are very happy as well as the architects because, after months of discussion, we bring the discussion to something new. The question is how to create new imagery for the people.

JPV | Economics is very important sometimes. Of course if the money doesn't allow new imagery, then all this is not possible. At the School of Nantes we convinced them that the new was possible, we said we could do three times the square meters more for the same projects in order to have a nice, comfortable building.

MF| *What if there is no possibility of discussion?*
JPV | We lose!
AL | However, before we lose, we do the projects and in them we try to leave places open for further discussion. We try to leave some parts of the project undefined, to create some basis permitting a different drift or opening.
JPV | Sometimes there is no discussion. This happened with some developers and the collaboration ended very quickly. We try to have a good work environment, without arguing. We would have liked to create a good team; it could have been an exciting adventure, where you have some risks for which you know you will find solutions. This is a sort of friendly attitude but with some developers it hasn't worked. Of course, we take money into account, luxury when needed but, in our experience, what they are looking for is standard features and categories. When this happens, we are not comfortable: why should we give up the maximum f it is possible to achieve it? For me it is OK that developers get their benefits, but inhabitants should also have benefits in terms of quality of space.

MF| *Do you discuss the image of the building with the client?*
AL | It has never been an issue.
JPV | But we do not discuss it between us either! Image is the result of the process.
AL | During the second phase of the Palais of Tokyo, we didn't want to do rendering. We considered it was not necessary; we could not invent a possible scenography for a possible exhibition. The Minister of Culture was not happy with our attitude. We were even accused of having a big ego. Finally, we explained our reasons; we asked for a meeting with him in the building to explain the project directly on the spot. When it took place, he understood the project very well and its reasons.
JPV | For example, in the house in the forest, because of regulations, we had to be 50 m from the sea, 4 m from each neighbour and the height was limited, so we followed the slope of the land. After that we decided we wanted to walk on the plot as if there was no house, so it was clear we would need some pilotis. The house was already situated very high, and after that we said we didn't want to cut down any trees and we didn't want to ruin the sand dunes. And the project was drawn!
AL | And the height of the floor had to be defined in such a way that we could see the sea just above the bushes.
JPV | We might say the form we like is that given by the maximum. In Nantes it is the maximum possible, in the Café the maximum possible, nearly everywhere it is the maximum possible.

MF| *Have you ever received any specific request from clients? For example, regarding materials, maybe wood instead of steel or concrete?*
JPV | No, but if someone says he would prefer wood as a material, for me that would be OK. I would just explain that if the building is made of wood, it will be more expensive.
AL | It would be OK if it were possible.
JPV | We don't mind so much about that. I would not say we like concrete or steel more than other materials.
AL | I remember there was a discussion like this in Cap Ferret. In that case, we were not very comfortable building with wood in a forest. It was ambiguous. The client understood the reason and he accepted the solution we gave.
JPV | It was cheaper to use steel and the dimensions of the profile were much smaller. It was interesting for us to see the big trunks crossing the house that were massive while the structure of the house was thinner. We also liked the contrast between the movement of the trees in the wind and the stability of the steel.
AL | We didn't like the idea of cutting down some trees while others would have been standing in the house. We use wood more for partitions, ceilings or to line the walls.

MF| *How do you choose the materials for the buildings?*
JPV | It depends on cost, performance, the span between the columns, whether the situation lets us use pre-fabricated elements or not.
AL | For example, for many projects it was interesting that in the dwellings there was no structure inside, no walls. That is why we worked on a span of 9/10 meters. We look for the most relevant construction system to fit the intentions.
JPV | In some projects, we chose components, like pre-cast slabs, that are usually used for offices, not for housing. Currently in France a bedroom is 3 m wide, a living room can be 5 m, so you have concrete elements that work on a 3 or 5 m span. We prefer systems that let us directly have a 10 m span. Then the secondary partitions come in. Sometimes between the units you have concrete walls, but we do not like them, we do not need them. We like the system of frames, the minimum number of columns, going back to Maison Domino, and partitions where needed.
AL | It could be wood, or steel. In some cases the contractor made it less expensive with walls in between than columns, but what we didn't accept was changing the span.

MF| *So it seems you never changed the material just for the appearance of the building...*
JPV | Well, for example at Cap Ferret we used corrugated aluminium for the reflection effect. In the Vienna Café we used tiles for the reflection of the light. Transparency is also very important.
JPV | The first choice is of structures, then there is the choice of façade, which is often defined by maximum transparency and opening. That is why we use a lot of glass sliding doors from the ground to the ceiling. The material for the winter gardens was something different because we didn't need the same efficiency in terms of insulation; it's even better if it is less waterproof than a glass door. The aesthetic aspect comes from the way the elements are manufactured or designed.
JPV | At the Nantes school there are three types of handrails to protect the balcony. First we made an infrastructure, a path connecting with the top, after that we defined a sort of maximum space closed by an industrial rail made of steel elements 10 cm each. Then the loft was ready to accommodate the school of architecture, and we created the intermediate floors and new floors, ceilings and glass balconies. As you can see, there is the brutal, solid level first, then the intermediate level that is industrial and finally the top one that is very residential.

MF | *In this way you really affirm the process and stress the layers ...*
AL | It is a result of different criteria including efficiency, functions, costs, aspects, solidity. It is the best balance between them.
JPV | The process at the Café in Vienna was strange. There was this old horse stable with three vaults and another little space where at the beginning we thought we would place the kitchen and the toilets. This space was not available at a certain point because a larger project for the site was coming. Therefore, we had to find a place for the kitchen and the toilets within the same vault volumes. We already had the idea of the ceiling covered by tiles that was interesting because of the historic references to Turkish presence in Austria. At that time, there was a political discussion by the right-wing parties to banish the Turks from Austria; it was in the time of Jörge Haider. We had already imagined the ceiling covering the three vaults, but suddenly we had to divide the three vaults into two parts: two vaults for the restaurant and one for the kitchen and toilets. We decided to have one big vault anyway; similar to something that could have existed in the past. We wanted to give the impression that at a certain moment a man who wants to make a restaurant divides the space with concrete blocks, leaving the tiles on both sides. In fact, the tiles were prepared before. Finally, we built the wall, we left 20 cm for the tiles. We wanted visitors to understand that the tiles existed long before the walls.

AL | And if they take away the walls the ceilings are continuous and complete.

MF *In this sense "re-invent" does not just involve what there was in the past but also what can be re-invented for the future. I think this is one of the most interesting parts of your work, you design architecture ready to be changed or reinvented in the future.*

JPV | It is also to tell a story, in the case of Vienna we tell a story. A story to be continued, a story that can be changed. The Palais de Tokyo also works like that. We tell a story to explain something, people may also give a different interpretation, but the story can be continued.

MF *I was thinking about a newbuild, where you create a new story ready to accept other stories in the future. Normally architecture tries to create relations with the past, it builds the present but sometimes has difficulty in imagining what the future will be. Obviously, there is a complex discussion about types, that is one of the aspects characterizing the history of architecture. How can we maintain the character of architecture but at same time be ready for different uses or transformation for the future?*

JPV | This is very interesting in housing. What we were asked to do was to make type 3, type 4 and type 1 with spatial organization of the rooms; think, however, about historic fabric, it is tissue. You have rooms, and people sometimes use one, sometimes two, there may be six rooms and people use two rooms or can use one room and another two at a higher level. This disappeared. We like this idea of tissue of spaces with different qualities, small, full of light, damp, matt, dark… A sort of fabrication of spaces that contains new spaces or old ones, new spaces complementary to old ones. It is about spatial changes.

Exibition Re-invent, Lacaton & Vassal, Torre San Giovanni, Alghero, 3-14 June 2014

editorial series:
Sustainable and affordable housing

editor in chief:
Massimo Faiferri

scientific-editorial committee:
Enric Batlle
Gonçalo Byrne
Anne Lacaton
Joe Noero
Federico Soriano
Jean Philippe Vassal

http://housing.aaamaster.it/

for info please contact:
DADU, Dipartimento di Architettura, Design e Urbanistica,
Palazzo del Pou Salit - Piazza Duomo 6, 07041 Alghero (SS).
e-mail aaamaster@uniss.it
www.architettura.uniss.it/ita/Didattica/Master

Collegio dei docenti Master "Sustainable and affordable housing"

Direttore del Master
Massimo Faiferri - Università di Sassari

Collegio del Master
Valter Caldana, Universidade Presiteriana Mackenzie Sao Paulo
Arnaldo Cecchini- Università di Sassari
Enrico Cicalò - Università di Sassari
Josep Mias Gifrè - Università di Sassari
Alessandro Plaisant - Università di Sassari
Ignasi Perez Arnal - Visiting professor presso l'Università di Sassari
Pedro Rodrigues, Universidade Tecnica de Lisboa
Silvia Serreli - Università di Sassari
Stefan Tischer- Università di Sassari

Docenti Tutor
Samanta Bartocci
Mauro Cossu
Filippo De Dominicis
Jacopo Galli
Fabrizio Pusceddu

Sustainable and affordable housing is an international book series founded with the aim of conveying the studies, research and cultural initiatives developed within the international Master's Degree Level 2 of the same name set up at the Department of Architecture, Design and Urbanism of the University of Sassari, in cooperation with the Facultade de Arquitectura of the Universidade Tecnica de Lisboa, the Universidade Presbiteriana of Sao Paulo and the Autonomous Region of Sardinia - Department of Labour, Vocational Training, Cooperation and Social Security.

The series uses a text evaluation system based on an anonymous peer-review by lecturers of the Publisher's Research Committee.

The creation of this series has been possible thanks to the contribution of:

Re-Invent
Reuse and transformation in Lacaton & Vassal's architecture

Author
Massimo Faiferri

Editorial Director
Alessandro Martinelli

Published by
LIStLab
info@listlab.eu
listlab.eu

Art Director & Production
Blacklist Creative, BCN
blacklist-creative.com

Photographs
© Philippe Ruault

ISBN 9788899854171

**Printed and bound
in the European Union,**
January 2018
December 2021 (re-print)

All rights reserved
© of LIStLab edition;
© of the author's texts;
© of the author's images;

series **sustainable and affordable housing collection**

No part of this book may be reproduced, stored in a retrieval system, or transmitted in any form or by any means, including electronic, mechanical, photocopying, microfilming, recording or otherwise without written permission from the publisher.

Sales, Marketing & Distribution
distribution@listlab.eu
listlab.eu/en/distribuzione/

For more information concerning Listlab's Scientific Boards please visit the webpage:
listlab.eu/en/board/

LIStLab is an editorial workshop, based in Europe, that works on contemporary issues. LIStLab not only publishes, but also researches, proposes, promotes, produces, creates networks.

LIStLab is a green company committed to respect the environment. Paper, ink, glues and all processings come from short supply chains and aim at limiting pollution. The print run of books and magazines is based on consumption patterns, thus preventing waste of paper and surpluses. LIStLab aims at increasing the responsibility of authors and the market, towards a new publishing culture based on smarter resource management.